GW01046533

John Michell is a dedicated schola[...]
and rediscovering the wisdom of [...]
The Flying Saucer Vision, The View [...]
in which he explains his fascinating and remarkable conclusions, caused a
sensation when they were first published and have subsequently become
international bestsellers.

Also by John Michell and available in Abacus

THE VIEW OVER ATLANTIS
CITY OF REVELATION

John Michell

THE FLYING SAUCER VISION
VISION

The Holy Grail Restored

ABACUS edition published in 1974
by Sphere Books Ltd
30/32 Gray's Inn Road, London WC1X 8JL

First published in Great Britain
by Sidgwick and Jackson Limited 1967
Copyright © John F. Michell 1967

ISBN 0 349 12319 5

This book is sold subject to the condition that it shall not,
by way of trade or otherwise, be lent, re-sold, hired out or
otherwise circulated without the publisher's prior consent in
any form of binding or cover other than that in which it is
published and without a similar condition including this
condition being imposed on the subsequent purchaser

Set in Monotype Times

*Printed in Great Britain by Cox & Wyman Ltd,
London, Reading and Fakenham*

Acknowledgments

Acknowledgments are made to the following for permission to reproduce illustrations used in this book.

Figures 1, 4 and 5 and Plate IV, Cambridge University Press.

Plate I, Mr and Mrs Allen Watkins; Plate II, Ashmolean Museum, Oxford; Plate V, Weidenfeld and Nicolson Limited; Plate VI, Department of the Environment, Crown Copyright; Plate VII, The Dean of Winchester; Plate VIII, Exposition Press Inc., New York; Plate IX, Routledge and Kegan Paul Limited; Plates X and XI, American Philosophical Society, Philadelphia; Plates XII and XIII, Hutchinson Publishing Group Limited; Plate XIV, James Clarke and Co. Limited; Plate XV, Mr Alfred Watkins and Hereford City Library.

Contents

List of Plates

Introduction to First Edition

It is now more than twenty years ago since people first began to notice the strange objects in the sky. By night bright lights were appearing overhead, moving rapidly like comets or the great fiery dragons so often seen in the past; by day they were seen as flying discs or globes. Newspapers called them flying saucers.

There was something about these objects and the stories connected with them that caused immediate excitement, and a rumour quickly spread that they were the spacecraft of intelligent beings from outside the earth. The claim by George Adamski, that he had seen one at close quarters in the Californian desert and spoken with its occupants, was followed by the publication of numerous books and articles by people with similar experiences, and it was not long before a popular tradition had become established about the creatures from space and their message to men on earth. The effect of all this, together with the official attitude that the objects were illusory or explicable as balloons, comets and the like, was to make the whole question of flying saucers seem rather ridiculous. Yet the rumours persisted. So many apparently reliable witnesses reported seeing flying saucers that the phenomenon could no longer be ignored. In some form, whether it was on a physical or a psychical plane, there could be no doubt that the strange apparitions in the sky had some actual existence.

As more people became aware of the flying saucer problem, it became evident that some scientific explanation was needed. But since official sources merely denied any knowledge of the mysterious flying objects (although the American and other governments had set up departments to study them) and since the objects themselves seemed to obey no known physical laws, a scientific approach to the problem was hardly possible. Attempts at analysing the facts apart from the legend which has grown up around flying saucers have been, perhaps, even less revealing of the true nature of these objects than the fantasies of writers such as Adamski. An investigation into the flying saucer problem is now being carried out for the US Government at Colorado University. But such projects are only undertaken with the object of finding conclusions comprehensible in scientific terms, and there is no indication that flying saucers can be measured in this way. It is even possible that they are not part of the one scale of space and time of which we are aware, but belong to an order of existence of which we have no conception. An attempt to apply our limited scientific system to the analysis of these objects may therefore be meaningless.

Since during the whole course of the post-war history of flying saucers few facts have emerged likely to impress or be of use to scientists, there appears to be only one way left by which we may come to understand something of their meaning: through the flying saucer legend. Since the first appearance of flying saucers an enormous amount of folklore has grown up around them. New ideas and old beliefs have been given a definite expression in the legend of the flying discs. People have recalled strange incidents from the past: blocks of ice falling from cloudless skies, showers of frogs and fishes, strange creatures appearing in different parts of the world, people vanishing. Stories such as these have become associated with the flying saucer phenomenon and reinterpreted as the result of flying saucer activity. At the same time it has become evident that flying saucers themselves are by no means new. A great many reports from the nineteenth century and earlier appear to refer to flying objects of the same sort as are seen today. In fact it appears from the works of Roman, Greek and Egyptian writers that the phenomenon was known in times of the remotest antiquity. Even the popular interpretation of flying saucers, that they are the spacecraft of an extra-terrestrial race, is nothing new, for in the earliest legends of mythology the flying vehicles of the gods are described in the same way, as wheels or winged discs. It may therefore be possible, by finding out how the strange flying objects were interpreted in the past, to achieve some understanding of the significance today. In doing this we shall have to reconsider some of the commonly accepted assumptions about the meaning behind the themes of mythology.

The time when the critical step was taken in human psychical evolution, when men first received the conception of the possibility of a higher cultural existence, is historically within our reach, for it is illustrated in the stories of original mythology. The more we study it, the more likely it seems that this step was taken suddenly, possibly as a result of some outside influence. Evolution has clearly not taken place as a smooth, inevitable process, but in a series of clearly defined moves, each occurring at one short moment of time. One of these moments must have been that of the first appearance of life on earth, though whether this was the result of some reaction on earth itself, or whether it was introduced from outside, is impossible to know. Of the other great moment, when men first achieved the expanded way of thought necessary for progress towards a civilisation, we have some record in mythology, and from this source we learn that the momentous step forward was taken through the appearance on earth of a superior race, the gods. The lessons learnt from that time have survived, sometimes embedded in the culture of the great civilisations of the past, sometimes guarded by more or less secret dynasties of priests and scholars in, for instance, the Druid colleges and certain remote monasteries of the East. In this way we have reached the present critical moment in the history of our civilisation, when no further significant progress seems possible within the existing system, when to many people our only hope of development and even survival seems to lie in the achievement of a new, higher vision, whatever form this may take. It may be that flying saucers today, as at the time of our last great vision, when they were revealed as the vehicles of the gods, are a portent of a further evolutionary step to be brought about through the working of some influence from outside the earth.

It is remarkable to what extent the flying saucer legend has incorporated former beliefs and superstitions, some of which were apparently moribund and others embedded for centuries in Christian mythology. Among them are the belief that people can vanish from the face of the earth, often for pursuing too zealously certain lines of inquiry into secret affairs; the belief in another race of men-like creatures, occasionally seen on earth but belonging to a different order of existence from our own; the tradition of the gods from the sky and of the sacred mandala, the winged disc bringing both gifts and destruction, and finally the expectation of an approaching millennium, when another order of life will appear on earth.

That all these themes and legends should reappear at this time and cluster round the image of the flying saucer is an indication of the

11

vividness with which the recent portents in the sky have acted on people's minds. Flying saucers may have an entirely physical existence like ours, although using forces of which we are not yet aware. But this seems unlikely in view of their enigmatic behaviour. More probably they belong, like ghosts, to another order of matter. Some aspects of their existence are perceptible to us, for they leave certain physical traces. Moreover the changes which have already taken place due to the psychical effect of their appearance are incalculable. But scientists' inability either to dismiss or explain the flying saucer phenomenon must encourage the view that they have a nature and meaning outside our experience, that their coming is a small part of some approaching vision with which we shall soon be confronted.

Since we can hardly speculate upon events in the future, which may, in any case, be outside the range of our present vision and means of expression, our only approach to the meaning of the portents now appearing in the sky is by finding out what was known or thought about them in the past. The tradition of the circular airship of the gods has survived in religious practices and monuments, in mythology and folklore. If we compare its meaning in the past with the meaning which the new flying saucer legend is beginning to have for us today, some pattern may emerge. We may begin to suspect that, by the natural course of some great cycle of time, we have come to the brink of an experience of similar magnitude to that which attended the earlier flying saucer vision.

Introduction to Second Edition

Since 1967 when *The Flying Saucer Vision* was first published, the reported activity of mysterious objects in the sky has continued much as before, while all attempts at finding a scientific explanation or proof of any physical cause of the phenomenon have continued unavailing. The author is still asked whether he believes in flying saucers (a question it needs steady nerves to deal with), and still replies that he believes in the *phenomenon* on the undeniable evidence of its *effect*; for anyone who studies this flying saucer business soon comes to realise that the effect on contemporary ideas of the reports and legends accumulating around the phenomenon has been scarcely less revolutionary than would have been produced had an alien spacecraft chosen to land publicly on – the spot once favoured for this revelation – the White House Lawn. It now seems that Jung was right when in 1959 he identified the strange 'things seen in the sky' as portents of 'long-lasting transformations of the collective psyche'. The evidence for this is that throughout its post-war history the flying saucer phenomenon and its literature have been associated with a change in prevailing modes of thought so radical that it amounts to a change in the popular cosmology, that is, in the way people understand the universe and their place in it.

As far as twenty years ago, when the first flying saucer books were appearing, their authors, even those who appeared excessively naïve or half-mad, and however improbable the experiences they claimed, were united by a sort of common philosophy, at that time considered unorthodox or even lunatic, yet now becoming ever more generally accepted by the respectable and responsible as the only alternative to the materialistic philosophy that threatens to destroy the earth, people and all. Many of the received ideas of the modern 'Save the Earth' movements were first expressed in flying saucer literature by such writers as Hunt Williamson, Fry, Kraspedon, Desmond Leslie,

Brinsley le Poer Trench, Arthur Shuttlewood etc., pioneers to whom acknowledgments are due – rather than expected – from the critics who ridiculed their ideas before plagiarising them. Several of these writers have incurred derision and personal spite on account of the prophetic content of their works, and it is ironic that it is only recently, now that the subjects they dealt with have become freely discussed, that the German author of a best-selling flying saucer book should write as his opening sentence the boastful declaration, which Colin Wilson has called the first of the book's many lies: 'It took courage to write this book and it will take courage to read it.'

Returning to the matter of flying saucers, and leaving aside for the moment questions of whether or in what form flying saucers exist, the most significant aspect of the whole phenomenon is its legend, the associated ideas that have arisen with it. Specifically, it has led directly to the rediscovery of items of ancient knowledge and facts about the past, long neglected yet of most timely relevance to the present. *The Flying Saucer Vision* was heavily mocked in the archæological press for drawing attention to an apparent connection between scenes of flying saucer activity and places of ancient sanctity. At that time little had been heard since the war of the strange archæological theory of 'the old straight track', said by its discoverer, Mr Alfred Watkins, to link in dead-straight alignments the sacred sites of neolithic Britain. The whole idea was thoroughly and almost unanimously condemned by archæologists as a baseless fantasy, and had it not been for the intuition of an English amateur of folklore, archæological and flying saucer studies, Tony Wedd, that there might be a connection between the centres of activity and straight flight paths mentioned in flying saucer reports and the alignments of ancient sites, Watkins's discovery might long have remained unknown and uninvestigated. As it turned out, the impetus given to this research by the flying saucer connection was sufficient to bring about a re-examination of Watkins's evidence, with the result that his theory is now widely accepted together with its corollary of scientifically advanced civilisation in prehistoric Britain. This introduces another aspect of the flying saucer enigma, the matter of whether the objects seen in the sky are motivated by a form of cosmic or terrestrial natural energy. Wilhelm Reich, the scientist and martyr, from his own observations of flying saucers believed this to be the case, and articles in Mr Bowen's *Flying Saucer Review* present evidence of a link between flying saucer activity and disturbances or anomalies in the field of terrestrial magnetism. It is therefore interesting that investigation of prehistoric civilisation suggests that its sacred places, its centres of ritual and science, were also located by magnetic considerations in relation to geological faults and underground watercourses; moreover that the ancients were not only aware of the earth's magnetic flow as influenced by the heavenly bodies, but made use of it for purposes of fertility and magic. That so many writers have been led on from an initial interest in flying saucers to enquire into the secrets of the ancient world is another example of the curious parallel between the two subjects.

It may be, as some have thought, that there is an intelligence behind the flying saucer phenomenon, concerned by this means to draw human attention to aspects of earth and cosmos which modern men have too long ignored. The matter is speculative and highly mystical. But the remarkable fact is that flying saucers have actually had this effect. Whether or not it was so intended, the mere rumour of their appearance in the skies throughout the world has influenced the direction of science and inspired new ideas and new discoveries.

As to whether and in what way flying saucers exist, an excellent analysis of the subject is provided in John Keel's *UFO's: Operation Trojan Horse*, the last two chapters in particular, a most important contribution to the study of the flying saucer phenomenon. Keel's first approach to the subject was as a sceptical journalist, then he became convinced of the reality and importance of flying saucer sightings, began to see them himself, to have strange psychic or psychotic experiences in connection with them, even to the point of receiving personal communications and guidance, and finally came to understand that the phenomenon is less physical than mental, that it is a sign of occult powers in the universe which control the human mind and may, if allowed to do so, utterly possess it to the destruction of the individual so possessed. A dramatic example of the effects of such possession, quoted by Keel, is the case of the Brazilian, Dino Kraspedon, author in 1959 of *My Contact with Flying Saucers*, a strange and impressive book, containing, in addition to precise explanations of how flying saucers navigate, a revolutionary message from the space people themselves about how atheism and materialistic technology is destroying the earth and misleading people as to the true nature of the universe. Kraspedon, under his real name,

15

Felix, later gained a reputation as a radical prophet, foretelling on television the assassinations of Martin Luther King and Robert Kennedy and announcing, also correctly, that a wave of terrorism would hit Sao Paulo in 1968. When in that year newspaper offices, police headquarters, the American Consulate and much else were blown up, Felix's fame as a prophet rose high, until he himself was arrested as the terrorist leader. At his trial Felix declared himself a Venusian agent, acting on behalf of the flying saucers which would shortly invade and conquer the earth.

Many, perhaps all writers on the subject of flying saucers have had some experience of the ordeals, both delightful and dangerous, which Keel passed through successfully and Kraspedon did not. There is a strange law of nature by which the universe obligingly produces confirmatory manifestations in response to thoughts and ideas projected onto it. In other words, reality is affected by the way in which one perceives it. Whoever makes a concentrated study of any subject finds his obsessions reflected in the world around him. There is the familiar phenomenon of the 'library angel', so called by Arthur Koestler, who rewards the devoted student with beneficial coincidences in the form of books, references and information that are brought to his attention at the very time he needs them. And there is the corresponding opposite principle, supplying disasters and obstructions, which may also be invoked by an excited imagination. Students of occultism, cosmology and such elusive phenomena as flying saucers are, for better or worse, especially susceptible to these influences. As Keel points out, many in recent years have been first inspired and then cruelly deceived by the forces stirred up in the course of their study, whether these be taken for spacemen or the spirits of the dead. Yet by the same forces others have been informed and initiated, the effect of the hermetic spirit depending on the recipient's sense of proportion.

The situation when *The Flying Saucer Vision* was written was that to mention in general conversation the subject of flying saucers was to invite ridicule and suspicion even from educated liberal company. It was as if something about the thing threatened the prevailing hierarchy of ideas, in which scepticism was held with the tenacity of a religious faith. The purpose of the book was, first, to point out the similarities between modern flying saucer manifestations and corresponding elements in ancient mythology – to emphasise the ortho-

16

doxy of the subject; second, to support Jung's warning, repeated by other early flying saucer writers, of coming changes 'which are in accord with the end of an era'. Flying saucers, whatever else they may be, are portents – signs and instruments of change. To become involved in the subject is to come under the influence of the forces by which change is directed, and it is for this reason that the subject has been so unsusceptible to investigation by scientific methods. Yet it is a personal belief that the value of flying saucer studies has so far generally been underestimated, that behind the phenomenon is something real and important, that what is being indicated is an essential though long neglected aspect of natural law, without knowledge of which human philosophy is incomplete and lasting civilisation impossible.

Those who like mysteries with simple solutions may find these conclusions excessively mystical, preferring more sturdy fantasies of itinerant spacemen. However, since every apparently sensible theory of flying saucer origins is mocked by the varied and fantastic nature of the evidence, it remains only to approach the subject on its own terms, to unite the phenomenon with its legendary associations, ancient and modern, and to experience the vital influence of an eternal symbol reborn.

Apart from this Introduction and a new photograph substituted for an unclear one, the text of this book, unchanged, is a genuine artefact of 1967.

CHAPTER ONE

The Flying Saucer Age

In 1959 towards the end of his life, C. G. Jung made a remarkable statement. Referring to the widespread reports of strange objects seen in the sky he said,

'These rumours, or the possible physical existence of such objects, seem to me so significant that I feel myself compelled, as once before when events were brewing of fateful consequence for Europe, to sound a note of warning. I know that, just as before, my voice is much too weak to reach the ear of the multitude. It is not presumption that drives me, but my conscience as a psychiatrist that bids me fulfil my duty and prepare those few who will hear me for coming events which are in accord with the end of an era. As we know from ancient Egyptian history, they are symptoms of psychic changes that always appear at the end of one Platonic month and at the beginning of another. They are, it seems, changes in the constellation of psychic dominants, of the archetypes, or "gods" as they used to be called, which bring about, or accompany, long lasting transformations of the collective psyche. This transformation started within the historical tradition and left traces behind it, first in the transition from the age of Taurus to that of Aries, and then from Aries to Pisces, whose beginning coincides with the rise of Christianity. We are now nearing that great change which may be expected when the spring-point enters Aquarius. It would be frivolous of me to conceal from the reader that reflections such as these are not only exceedingly unpopular, but come perilously close to those turbid fantasies which becloud the minds of world-improvers and other interpreters of "signs and portents". But I must take this risk, even if it means putting my hard-won reputation for truthfulness, trustworthiness, and scientific judgement in jeopardy. I can assure my readers that I do not do this with a light heart. I am, to be quite frank, concerned for all those who are caught unprepared by the events in question and disconcerted by their incomprehensible nature. Since, so far as I know, no one has yet felt moved to examine and set forth the possible psychic consequences of this foreseeable change, I deem it my duty to do what I can in this respect. I undertake this thankless task in the expectation that my chisel will make no impression on the hard stone it meets.'

The context in which these words appear – they are taken from his book, *Flying Saucers, A Modern Myth of Things Seen in the Skies* – gives some clue to what Jung had in mind when he spoke of 'great changes' to come. Our peculiar dilemma at the present time is that, while scientists tell us that in all probability conditions in millions of other bodies in the universe are suitable for the existence of life as we know it on earth and there is no reason to doubt that it has in fact evolved elsewhere, we have somehow yet been unable consciously to accept this probability and to speculate what it might mean to us and our future. The idea of extra terrestrial-intelligent beings appears to be too large a subject to fit into our present system of thought. It is therefore either ridiculed or ignored.

The changes which Jung foresaw will come about as the limits within which we think expand to allow the existence of extra-terrestrial life. The arbitary framework which limits our way of thinking, our western liberal-humanist system, based on the Hebrew-Christian tradition and seemingly confirmed by the superior technology which enabled us to exploit and patronise the natives of our colonies, has evolved to its limits and is now approaching a state of decadence. The next stage, a moral and intellectual collapse, which will eventually be followed by the birth of a new order of thought, could, as Jung warned, have disastrous consequences. These can only be avoided if we can prepare ourselves for events which may shortly happen, events which may involve learning to understand that we are not alone in the universe, that we may even be, as the American writer Charles Fort, said 'property', already the object of study by an alien people.

In our sudden state of unpreparedness the sudden forcible introduction of such an idea into our conscious minds would be calamitous. The science of anthropology is still undeveloped, but we know

now what happens to primitive people when they are suddenly brought into contact with an alien culture unattainably more advanced, a contact which often results in their complete demoralisation, a refusal even to breed and their consequent extinction. If intelligent life has developed in other parts of the universe, it is mathematically certain that in some cases it has reached a considerably higher level – perhaps by millions of years – than that which we have so far attained. In this case the problems of space travel, with which we are just beginning to concern ourselves, would in those other centres of life long ago have been solved. Many people suspect, not without some evidence, that we have for many ages been the object of study by an extra-terrestrial force, a study which is now approaching a climax. Up to now the anthropological knowledge of the extra-terrestrials which they may have gained through their experiences on earth in the remote past, has kept them from presenting themselves to us and our emerging civilisation in open form. How long this state of affairs will last depends on the length of time it will take us to prepare ourselves to receive them.

The signs are, however, that some form of encounter with an alien force will not long be delayed. It seems likely that we are at this moment undergoing a process of preparation for this event. Gradually our minds are being adapted to a point where we will begin to expect and desire a contact with extra-terrestrials. When this state is achieved, the next great step in human history will be taken, shaping the new Aquarian age which we are now entering.

The belief that we are in some way warned of events to come and even actively prepared to accept them is nothing new. This idea was the basis of all previous civilisations. Enormous energy was expended to make sure that signs and portents in the sky were accurately interpreted. The science of astronomy and its practical extension, astrology, were studied to the exclusion of almost all the other branches of knowledge which make up our present civilisation. To this end the building of Stonehenge was undertaken, a labour which the astronomer Gerald S. Hawkins compares in scale to the American space programme. The civilisations of Central America were ruled above all by observation of the skies and the application of the knowledge learnt from them. Jacques Soustelle in his book on the Aztecs says,

'From the Mayas, who seem to have been positively hypnotised by time and its majestic passage, onwards, all the civilised nations of Mexico and Central America worked out complex chronological systems, and this for two purposes: the first was to find fixed points in order to understand and foresee the succession of natural phenomena, the seasons, and the movements of the stars, and so to regulate the rites that were necessary to their proper sequence; the second was to determine the fate of each man and the fortunes of each undertaking by means of a body of portents which made up a coherent whole quite as "scientific" for those people as our rational explanations of the world are for us.'

It is easier to explain the interest which former civilisations took in the patterns in the sky as a traditional part of an atrophied social order than it is to explain the same interest shown today in our society where there is no formal education in such matters. Yet there is no denying that popular interest in astrology, horoscopes and the like is, if anything, increasing. It is possible to see in this a recognition of some kind of external influence in our affairs, or even the influence itself at work to prepare us for the changes we must now expect. By studying the direction in which this influence is leading it may be possible for a certain number of people to understand something of what these changes will involve and by forming a bridge between the two ages, present and future, mitigate to some extent the disasters they will bring.

A recent development in which some see an approaching revolution in our attitudes of thought is the increasingly wide interest in the use of drugs. Occurring at a time when no further progress seems possible within the present system, their appearance as 'deus ex machina' to expand the limits of experience is remarkably opportune. It is hardly likely that their development and use at this very time can be a matter of pure chance. The expansion of the conscious mind which many people have claimed as the result of experiments with drugs seems so in accord with the direction of our mental development, so desired and expected, that the influence of an external force in their introduction must be suspected. This desire for an enlightenment beyond the present bounds of our experience has led a Dutch doctor and certain of his followers to look for a permanent psychedelic experience by performing a trepanning operation on themselves, making an opening in the front part of the skull. Their assumption is that this operation, which is known to have been practised by certain members of vanished races in the past, including the mysterious pre-Incan race of South America, whose monumental signs to the gods in the sky have recently after thousands of years been rediscovered, can develop their awareness of forces with which these people were familiar. Whether or not any direct enlightenment is achieved by this means, there is no doubt that the appearance of increasing use of mind-expanding drugs has already influenced the development of our philosophy, opening the way to what may be an entirely new series of concepts.

The most dramatic, perhaps the most significant, indication of approaching change is the phenomenon of the strange objects seen in the skies, UFOs or flying saucers. Although it now appears that these objects have been seen at all times back to the remotest antiquity, their impact on our consciousness only took place after the war. What was at first taken to be a fantasy exaggerated by journalists and a convenient field for opportunist charlatans, is now becoming a serious study for people with scientific interests. Jung was one of the first to speculate on their meaning. In a curious way, he found, their coming had been expected and desired by a great many people. The 'meaningful coincidence' of their appearance during the uncertainties of the post-war period led him to conclude that their nature was more complicated than at first appeared. Of their physical existence he was convinced by the respectable character of many of the witnesses to them, and by other evidence, such as their appearance on radar screens. Yet he also found that they featured in the dreams of people who had never even heard of them. From this he suggested that they were in the nature of portents, both a warning and an actual part of the great changes he expected.

Far from dying down, as most people expected, flying saucer activity appears actually to be increasing. At present the only two groups of people who are actively conscious of them are those individuals who, for some reason, have interested themselves in the subject, and the governments of the world powers, who have each set up departments to study them. Yet by their appearance they have in some way altered things. People who deny their existence are still aware of them if only as a distant threat to the established order. They have become a symbol of the dramatic possibilities of space travel. Through them we have all become less sure of our unique position in the universe.

In all the years since we first became conscious of them, however, flying saucers have maintained their enigmatic character. There are no really good photographs of them; stories of their landing and of contact with their occupants have never been substantiated. It is just such objects as these, objects which we cannot really doubt but can still not actually prove or identify, that are ideally calculated to disturb the order of our thoughts, to put us into a state of mental anarchy which must precede the start of a new phase of our history.

CHAPTER TWO

The Flying Saucer Tradition

If the approaching changes which Jung predicted involve us in an entirely new experience and introduce new dimensions of philosophy, they must by their very nature be outside the present limits of our comprehension. Ideas of a totally different order from those in which we now deal, those for which there is yet no pattern or precedent within the terrestrial limit, are inexpressible in terms of language and therefore unattainable. Language can only apply within our historical experience. Pole in his commentary on Wittgenstein says, 'Our attitudes are embodied in our language and expressed in its grammar. Together they define the limits of discourse – limits beyond which we can not pass.' From this we can see the impossibility of obtaining an answer where we lack the language in which to frame the question. Conversely all problems of which we are aware have attainable solutions. (Socrates: Then he who does not know still has true notions of that which he does not know. Memo: he has). New concepts can only be realised by an expansion of language, and this expansion must result from some totally new order of experience.

Although every form of human development is limited to that which can conceive of attaining, there is no reason to doubt that our potential is capable of a sudden, marked expansion. For untold thousands of years, from the first appearance of the human race to the time when the first steps were taken towards a civilisation, men, the same as we are today, lived in a state of nature unable to imagine any possible change in their condition. Suddenly something happened, something which created such a violent shock that the trauma has remained with the human mind ever since. The event shifted the fulcrum of human intellect; it opened a vision whose existence had not only never been suspected, but could never have had any conceivable meaning had the event which exposed it not taken place.

25

Whatever caused this first great revolution was something hitherto extrinsic to the human mind. For uncounted ages men had lived on earth, experiencing all the adventures which a purely terrestrial existence could provide. Yet nothing had happened, no sequence of events had taken place which had caused the slight shift in vision necessary to the conception of civilisation. It is hard to believe that after all the ages of men's existence on earth some spontaneous reaction could have occurred, deriving solely from influences within the terrestrial limit, influences which must have been active throughout the whole of human experience, whereby men suddenly became aware of the possibility of creating a society. Far more acceptable is the open message of comparative mythology.

In this we have an unambiguous account of the first days of civilisation. The earliest myths describe the arrival on earth of an extra-terrestrial race, who, by their example altered the whole course of human history. Whoever these people were, their level of culture was so far outside men's comprehension at that time, that their sudden confrontation with the extra-terrestrials led to a revolutionary change in the whole pattern of human existence. This is the literal message of mythology, the only interpretation which resolves the many problems which it raises. Once we can accept the, at first sight, fantastic idea that our present culture is an inheritance from a former visit of people from space, a great deal of what is now obscure becomes clear. Besides providing the key by which we can interpret the myths and legends which form our early history and understand the meaning of certain symbols, petroglyphs and monuments of antiquity, the realisation that at some time in the past an extra-terrestrial race has appeared on earth helps us to understand something of the significance which the recent flying saucer manifestations will have for us in the future. The age we are now entering is in many ways similar to that which preceded the first arrival of the alien race, the gods. A study of that former time may therefore enable us to see the possible consequences of a confrontation with extra-terrestrial life in the future.

The time of our first enlightenment, the introduction of civilisation by the gods from space, may seem to be so remote that we have little chance of learning anything about it. But in fact the tradition of what happened at that time has remained strong up to the present day in the various myths and legends common to all parts of the world. The evidence of mythology provides a general account of the days when the gods were known on earth. At first it seems, their coming caused misery and chaos. Men became aware of things which before had been entirely inconceivable. From their primal state of innocence they became committed to the task of developing their newly realised potential to the full. Nothing was the same, there was no more certainty. In place of the old system which had once seemed to be an integral part of human existence, there now stretched an apparently endless prospect of continual progress with all the responsibilities and competition which it involved. Not unnaturally men looked back to the former times with a hopeless yearning for the golden age now irretrievably lost. For the minds which had been opened by the vision of the gods could never again be contracted.

In the period immediately preceding the arrival of the gods, men became aware of certain peculiar signs and portents in the sky. Fiery circles were seen by night, and by day flying discs passed overhead. The meaning of these phenomena was revealed when the objects came down to earth and were seen to be airships of a strange, unimaginably advanced race of people. Ever since that time men have been obsessed by the image of the circular flying vehicle and the god from space. The two figures are frequently shown together in the earliest illustrations to the legends of the gods' first arrival, which describe the divine race as descending to earth inside the flying disc.

The oldest and most powerful symbol of the Deity is that of a figure inside a wheel. This form was later conventionalised as the cross within the circle, examples of which are the Celtic cross, the cruciform church placed within the pre-Christian circular churchyard and the gold, cross-bearing discs of prehistoric Wessex burials. Another, purer form is that of the Lycian symbol, the three legs within the wheel which in the Isle of Man, where it appears on an ancient pillar cross, is said to represent Manannann, the giant god of the island who 'rolled on three legs like a wheel through the mist'. The swastika is similarly a corrupt symbol of the god within the spinning disc.

The earlier the inscription the more explicit is the figure of the god within the circular airship. On prehistoric Assyrian cylinders appears the figure of a man, presumably one of the divine race, descending to earth inside a disc, and the god Assur is shown in this way, upright against a wheel in the sky or issuing from it. In his hand he holds the gods' weapon, the flamethrower or thunderbolt. Early rock inscriptions show the god, Ahura Mazda, riding through the sky inside a circular vehicle or, in stylised form, as part of it. Indian gods are frequently depicted flying within an aerial disc. Vishnu, like Assur, spins through the sky in a wheel, launching thunderbolts to earth, and many other Indian deities, including the monkey god, Hanuman, have this striking association with the disc in the sky. Sometimes the god is shown running inside the rim of the wheel, a form which seems designed to indicate its spinning motion. The same conventional image of the sky god inside a spinning disc is found in many parts of the East and in Europe, appearing as the spokes of the divination wheel, or as the figure rising from the dome of Tibetan Buddhist temples.

Even though little research has yet been done on the question of possible visits to earth by extra-terrestrial life in the past, it is still surprising that the recurring image of the flying saucer in connection with the gods of antiquity has been so little remarked. The reason is partly because of the strength of the nineteenth century belief that the disc in the sky is always a symbol for the sun or moon. It is true that a cult for these and other heavenly bodies did later arise to complement or supplant the original worship of the actual gods. But the primary object of veneration was not the solar disc itself, but the god who rode it through the sky. The conception of the 'man in the moon' is extremely old and was once of real significance. It was only after the gods withdrew from earth that their cult, already transferred to the discs in which they travelled, became attached to the visible heavenly bodies. In Mexico and Egypt the gods only became associated with the sun after their time on earth was over. Re, the supreme god of Egypt, became the sun-god after he had left earth with the goddess Nut, who bore him up on her back in her form of a cow. Before that his vehicle, the 'eye of Re', had been the winged disc, the fearsome circle of fire which almost destroyed the rebellious human race. Like the disc of Vishnu, from which thunderbolts were launched to earth, the winged disc was both a vehicle and an instrument of war and had no original connection with the solar circle. It was only when open knowledge of the gods' flying discs was lost that their legend was transferred to the visible heavenly bodies.

In a search for an association between the ancient figure of the circle, mandala or flying disc and that of the flying saucer the vital clue is to be found in the legends of the dragon. This creature, together with its homologues, the serpent, lizard, crocodile, eel, worm, flying dog and other such monsters, stands in the mythological and poetic languages for the fiery disc in the sky. G. Elliot Smith in *The Evolution of the Dragon* lists the dragon's characteristics. It lives on the tops of mountains; it is associated with lakes, wells and pits in the earth; it guards valuable treasure and imparts knowledge to men; from it issue thunder and lightning; its light illuminates the earth by night. All these qualities link the dragon with the flying saucer. A Chinese legend quoted by D. Mackenzie in *Myths of Pre-Columbian America* further illustrates their association:

> 'When dark clouds covered the sky everywhere at night, a noise of thunder was heard in the north. . . . This was what people call a descent of the celestial dog. . . .
>
> It has a shape of a large moving star, and produces a noise.
>
> When it descends and reaches the earth, it resembles a dog.
>
> Whatever it falls upon becomes a flaming fire; it looks like a fiery light, like flames flaming up to heaven. . . .
>
> Thunder resounded in the north-west in a cloudless sky, and this was called a descent of the celestial dog. . . .
>
> The celestial dogs live on the tops of high mountains. . . .
>
> Their colour resembles that of the dragon.'

The use of the dragon image to describe mysterious flying objects persisted until recent times. One of the latest accounts was that of Prefect Scherer who in 1619 saw what he called a fiery dragon fly over a lake from a cave on Mount Pilatus in Switzerland. Even later, though more ambiguous, was the dragon of St Leonard's Forest in Sussex whose last appearance was during the nineteenth century. It is hardly an exaggeration to say that in a comparison of old and new legends the figures of the dragon and the flying saucer are invariably interchangeable.

The discovery that flying saucers, the fiery discs in the sky, were reported in the past as dragons or winged serpents reveals the significance of a great deal of previously obscure mythology and folklore in which these creatures figure. The extraordinarily vivid English dragon-killing legends, some of which are given in the last chapter of this book, and all those myths where the serpent is described as the airship of the gods, the vessel from which all human

29

benefits derive, can be seen as symbolic accounts of the early dealings between the gods and men.

The origin of the identification of the serpent with the flying saucer is to be found in the snake's characteristic habit of coiling into a circle or spiral. Irish folklore says that snakes travel long distances by putting their tails in their mouths and bowling along like a hoop. In this form they flew from the top of Croagh Patrick, the sacred mountain, when expelled by St Patrick, a legend later adapted to symbolise the suppression by the Christian Church of the old worship of flying gods. A memorial to this former religion can be seen in the beautiful spiral and circular motifs carved on the stones of New Grange in County Meath which together with the other great artificial hills of the neighbourhood formed a centre for the worship of the spinning discs in the sky.

One of the most explicit myths of the serpent as the airship of the gods occur among the Ainus, the aborigines of Japan. The goddess of fire, whose special responsibility was the earth, came down to help men. The heavenly serpent loved the goddess and offered to fly her down to the earth. He coiled into a spiral and descended with the goddess inside the circle of his body. Other serpents followed him coming down in the same way in the form of circles. They fell to earth so heavily that they have made depressions in the ground. These pits are still pointed out by the Ainu, who hold them in great reverence as the spots where the gods first arrived. This interesting legend has a connection with recent events and the development of a similar belief in England. In the summer of 1963 an object in the sky was seen during the night by a man living near Charlton in Wiltshire. The next morning a farmer of that village discovered a circular depression in his field of barley. The top soil and the growing crop within the circle had disappeared. An army investigation failed to solve the mystery of the sudden appearance of the pit which many people believe to have been caused by the landing of an object from the sky. In the same year similar pits were discovered at Flamborough Head, Dufton Fell in Westmorland and in a park in Southampton; others are said to have occurred in Ireland.

Further evidence of the identification of the serpent with the gods' sky vehicle can be found in early myths. There is hardly any mythological account of flight where the serpent does not appear, carrying or accompanying the flying god. The Egyptian winged disc, the 'eye of Re', has two fire-spitting uræus – serpents – one on each side. Of the Greek deities, Athene travelled to face the judgment of Paris in an aerial chariot drawn by two serpents; Kirke was carried from Kolchis in a similar vehicle, a team of winged serpents pulling it through the air; Aphrodite, impersonating Kirke, returned in the same chariot, and this same legend was also told of Medea. Later, Aphrodite made a flying wheel, binding to it an inyx or wryneck, a bird closely associated with the serpent because of its habit of hissing and twisting its neck. A number of paintings showing this wheel appear on Greek vases. Along the rim is a row of dots like the so-called portholes which feature in many flying saucer reports. The same dots are associated with the dragon or celestial dog of China, and with the dragon of British legend.

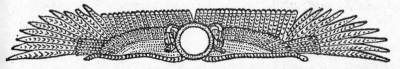

Fig. 1 *The Egyptian winged disc*

Another figure from Greek mythology who flew in a serpent chariot was Triptolemos, the god who first introduced wheat to earth. This early recognition of wheat as an alien plant is remarkable, since its origin has always been a mystery. There is no native plant anywhere on earth from which cultivated wheat appears to have descended. In this case it is hard to dismiss the idea that it was a gift to men, brought in to aid the development of human civilisation. The same story is told in Mexico of the god Quetzalcoatl (the feathered snake). Besides teaching man the arts of civilisation, the use of silver and masonry and the application of paint and decoration, Quetzalcoatl introduced the cultivation of corn. His vehicle, like that of Triptolemos, was a raft made of serpents. In a similar Polynesian legend the coconut plant first appeared from the head of an eel, a creature with the same legendary attributes as the serpent.

Gould in *Curious Myths of the Middle Ages* quotes an Icelandic saga in which the serpent plays much the same part as does the flying saucer in the books of the visionary American space travellers of the 1950s. Two young men, one Norwegian and one Danish, both called Eirek, set off on a long journey in search of Paradise. They passed through India and entered a gloomy forest emerging on a strange

31

shore where they saw the beginning of a bridge. Guarding the bridge was a great serpent. The Danish Eirek declined to advance any further, but the Norwegian walked right into the serpent's mouth and shortly afterwards found himself transported into the land of Paradise.

It proved to be a country as beautiful as that described by later visitors such as the American writers Adamski and Angelucci, and in no way dissimilar. One remarkable feature was a sort of tower hovering in the air a short distance above the ground and entered only by a thin ladder. Eirek climbed into the tower where he found food and enjoyed a refreshing sleep. In his dreams an angel appeared to him and told him that he would be taken back to earth, but that after ten years he would once more be received into Paradise. He was then transported by the serpent back to the place where he had left earth and after ten years in his own country ascended bodily to Paradise.

The clear identification of the serpent in this story with the modern concept of the flying saucer can be extended to cover almost every appearance of the serpent or dragon in mythology. Later by a natural development the serpent, the vehicle of the gods, came to stand for the gods themselves. This explains those myths which describe the serpent as the first introducer of the various forms of knowledge on which human civilisation is based. The most important of these, according to Lévi-Strauss the crucial step in the development of society, is the use and control of fire. All over the world there are legends that it was the serpent who first instructed men in this art. J. Meier in *Myths and Sagas of the Admiralty Islands* repeats the local story of how a woman took a serpent husband and by him had two children, a boy and a girl. The serpent then put away his wife and looked after the children himself. One day the serpent sent the children to catch some fish. When they came back with the fish he told them to cook it. 'We can not do so,' they said, 'for the sun is not up.' When the sun rose it warmed the fish, but they still had to eat it raw. 'You are just ghosts,' said the serpent. 'Crawl into my belly and bring out the fire you will find there.' The serpent opened his mouth and the boy crawled inside. He came out with fire and the serpent showed the children its use in cooking their food.

Many races, including the Polynesians, Andaman Islanders, Australians and Maoris, have a tradition that fire was originally stolen from the gods. In Greek mythology it was Prometheus who first brought fire to men. In historical terms Prometheus was either a member of the hybrid race, half man half god, or he was one of the renegade gods, those born on earth, who had more sympathy with men than with their own race. Early in his career Prometheus had tricked Zeus into accepting the more unattractive share of a feast by dressing it up to look the better. For this the supreme god had withheld from men the gift of fire. Prometheus stole it, that is he instructed men in its use in the same way as he introduced other knowledge for the development of civilisation, an action for which he received a terrible punishment. This important myth describes how the seeds were sown for the later conflicts between men and the gods.

All the myths such as these illustrate the antiquity of the belief that civilisation did not begin spontaneously on earth but was at one time introduced to men by an alien race. It was these people who were later remembered in the symbol of their airships, the serpent. As Bonwick says in *Irish Druids and the Old Irish Religion*, 'The serpent is certainly the token or symbol of an ancient race celebrated for wisdom'. The serpent was said to be responsible for the introduction of all the arts of civilisation, and to be the source of all wisdom. Knowledge of healing was first revealed by the serpent, and sacred snakes were kept in the temples of Aesculapius, the god of medicine, whose staff the serpent entwines. The Greeks and Romans believed that serpents uttered profound secrets in oracular form. Later German folklore included the belief that to eat a white serpent led to the acquisition of knowledge and power, and whoever ate the dragon's heart came to know all the secrets of the universe, the property of the gods.

Together with the tradition that the serpent revealed to men the path to civilisation there are other legends in which the serpent jealously guards his secrets, to obtain which he must be beguiled or killed. These reflect the second stage in the relationship between the gods and men, the period of disenchantment, when men, awakened to the opportunities which the coming of the gods had brought them, began to covet all the possessions of the gods, to which they seemed to owe their superiority. The desire to own the instruments of the gods led men several times to the brink of extinction, for whenever they came to acquire, by theft or imitation, those secrets which were far in advance of their own basic culture, they used them destructively to the danger of both men and gods. It was this which caused the friction between the two races which only ended with the gods' departure from earth.

They left behind them the legend of their wisdom and immortality, which was henceforth the object of men's yearning and quest. The men who had enjoyed close contact with the departed race, the heroes and demi-gods of mythology, devoted their lives to seeking out their former benefactors. They were looking for a return of the gods' flying discs, and the story of what they hoped to achieve is told in the legends of the killing of the dragon and the vision of the Grail. The Holy Grail, as it became in later Christian legend, was the vessel which men believed could give them all the secrets and powers of the gods, youth, love, knowledge and the ability to understand all that was then obscure. The lives of the heroes were devoted to a ceaseless hunt for this treasure. To obtain it, it was necessary to face the dragon who encircled it, to break into the flying disc and plunder its contents. This feat was performed by Peredur who, in a story from *The Mabinogion*, killed a great serpent and captured the ring on which it lay coiled. In the same way Hercules succeeded in capturing the inspiring apples of the Hesperides after he had killed their guardian, the serpent Ladon. The apple is commonly used to symbolise Ambrosia, represented as the food of the gods, through which men can achieve the expansion of the consciousness necessary for a vision of a higher way of life. There seems to be an archetypal belief that the apple can show men the way to a god-like state of wisdom and immortality. Voltaire's story of the discovery by Newton of gravity makes the apple the instrument of his enlightenment. In Avalon, the enchanted island where men stayed young for ever, apple trees grew in profusion. It is said that a crab apple was found in America which can induce hallucinations similar to those from psychedelic drugs. If this is so, the controlled eating of apples may have been a former mystic practice, designed like the modern use of the hallucinative mushroom to give men an insight into another world. This would explain the belief that the apple was the fruit of the Garden of Eden through which knowledge came, and the use of the apple to symbolise the secret of immortality which Hercules stole from the serpent, Ladon.

The serpent and the flying saucer occur together and have an identical character in the story quoted by Donald Mackenzie in

Indian Myth and Legend. The food of immortality, ambrosia or amrita, was coveted by men, but guarded by the flying disc of Vishnu, which destroyed all who sought to steal the cup containing it. Garuda, in this case like Prometheus a renegade god, set out to steal the amrita. It was kept on a high mountain, surrounded by a ring of flames and guarded by two serpents and a fiercely revolving disc, sharp-edged and brilliant. Garuda quenched the flames, killed the serpents and destroyed the disc. He then flew with the cup of amrita to the demons who had sent him on his mission, but before they could drink it, Indra snatched the cup up to heaven, and the demons were left desperately licking the spot on the ground where it had rested. In this is apparent the widely held belief that just one minute drop of the contents of the magic cup will give a man immortality and a knowledge of all the secrets of the gods.

In the period which followed the first appearance of the gods, the serpent, representing their circular airships, became the object of a messianic cult something like the cargo cult of the South Pacific. In the modern version of this movement its followers, primitive natives of the New Guinea area, are impressed by the riches which, they see, belong entirely to the white men. Such possessions, tinned food, clothes, radios and the like are so miraculous that they must have been sent by the gods, destined for the natives but stolen by the Europeans. Cargoes of the coveted goods are known to arrive in aeroplanes, and the natives come to believe that, if they can be intercepted, the benefits will come to them, to whom they rightfully belong. They therefore imitate the ways of the white men, erecting sticks like radio masts and clearing landing strips in the jungle. Magic rites are performed, all the cattle slaughtered and a feast prepared to welcome the expected cargo. When this fails to arrive and the cult dies, the natives are faced with starvation, having used up all their resources in the celebrations. The effect on primeval man of their first confrontation with the advanced beings from the sky must have been very like that which the sudden appearance of European civilisation had on the New Guinea natives. The shining dragon-disc was the object of the same desires as today are directed by the primitive people of New Guinea towards the aeroplane. The film *Mondo Cane* showed some of these natives building a fantastic model aeroplane on a huge scale in the hope that it would act as a decoy and attract the aeroplanes flying overhead. In the same way primitive men thousands of years ago, knowing the wealth to be found inside the sky discs, built circular mounds and arrangements of stones, whose form was visible only from the air. According to Mexican legends these circular shapes were only erected after the coming of Quetzalcoatl, the feathered serpent; in other words it was the appearance of flying discs in the sky that inspired them. These cargo cult monuments including the most famous of all, Stonehenge, the perfect flying saucer model, survive all over the world and their shape, that of the sacred circle, persisted well into Christian times long after its original meaning had been lost.

The legends of dragons as the guardians of fabulous treasure are a product of the times when men believed the discs in the sky to be the source of the gods' wealth. The wrath of the dragon when its treasure was stolen, as in the saga of Beowulf, is like that of Zeus when Prometheus stole fire for the benefit of men. In the former case, the dragon laid waste the country with his fiery breath, and so fierce was the destruction that the stone walls of Beowulf's fortress melted and fused together in a way reminiscent of the vitrified towers of Scotland, those mysterious monuments whose stones appear to have melted and run together as if a fierce blast of heat had been turned on to them from an object hovering directly overhead. Beowulf went out to meet the dragon, but its heat was so intense that only his iron shield saved him from being burnt. Another hero who joined him in the battle found his wooden shield useless and had to fight behind the shelter of Beowulf's. Together they wounded the dragon so that its fire abated and they were able to kill it. Beowulf later died from his injuries. The victory of the two men armed with a metal shield and swords may indicate that their enemy did not rely on this material. It is not inconceivable that the superior race had no practical use for metal. They were evidently a people who had mastered many of the natural laws that enabled them to travel through space and control the elements, but it is possible that metal had no place in their technology. It is hard for us to imagine space flight in a craft made of non-metallic material, but for anything other than short trips to our neighbouring planets a metal rocket, such as is now used, would be useless. For real space travel outside our solar system an entirely new concept, bearing no relation to our present means of propulsion, would be necessary. It is quite possible that a form of life which had solved the problems of journeying through space would have no interest in the human obsession with warfare, and, apart from the use of fire to deal with the attacks of men, would have no defence against quite simple weapons like metal swords. It may have happened that when men began to apply their newly acquired knowledge to their warlike purposes, they were able to defeat a people immeasurably superior in every way but that of making war. It was when the gods saw how powerless they were to prevent their secrets from falling into the hands of men, and realised how inevitably they would be used to spread destruction and greed, they decided to withdraw from earth.

Although in the course of time the treasure which the dragon guarded came to be thought of in terms of material wealth, gold and silver and jewels, the original object of men's desire was the food of the gods, the elixir of life. But the best known of all the dragon's treasures is the beautiful woman, rescued from her guardian by a human hero. There are two possible interpretations of this story, both of which may be correct in different circumstances. Either the heroine was a woman of the alien race, the 'swan maiden' or bride from the sky, referred to in another chapter, or she was a woman from earth, abducted by the gods in their need for human specimens. The Cretan minotaur was a figure, like the dragon, standing for the people from the sky. The labyrinth in which it lived, is a most significant figure of great complication, but in general it seems, like the spiral, to represent the spinning sky vehicle and to indicate the difficulties in the task of penetrating its mysteries. In this it is associated with the revolving glass towers of Celtic mythology, built by the gods on small islands. On the island of Crete, as on many others, the gods had made their home. It was here that the human specimens, perfect young men and women, were taken as sacrifice. This was done year by year until Theseus attacked and defeated the alien race, and released their human captives. The stories of Perseus and Andromeda and of Tristan and Isolde are among many others which refer either to the capture of a woman of the alien race by a native of earth or to the release of a human captive taken by the extra-terrestrials.

With the departure of the gods, dragons were no longer familiar objects on earth, but their memory was still kept alive by their intermittent reappearances. There is hardly any period of history which has not left the sort of records now called flying saucer reports. Sometimes the objects in the sky are described in the old form, such as the flying dragons which in 713 AD terrified the people of Northumbria. Later historical accounts tell of aerial globes, discs and moving lights. Desmond Leslie, one of the first to research on the subject, produced a list which gave twelve examples of such apparitions in the seventeenth and eighteenth centuries and included the huge flaming things seen over Worcester in 1661, the vast balls of fire which moved slowly over Edinburgh in 1750, the bright glows which appeared over Portugal in 1755 and over Switzerland six years later and the fighting balls and other flying objects which were seen in Basle, the incident later quoted by C. G. Jung. Similar descriptions occur in the works of earlier writers. Livy and Julius Obsequens give instances of strange moving lights and other objects over Italy reaching a climax in 218 BC when a flying shield was seen over Arpi, followed by reports of two moons in the sky, luminous flying ships, shining globes over Praeneste and strangers in white clothing appearing on earth. Perhaps most remarkable of all is the earliest known dragon-flying saucer report dating from the reign of the Egyptian King Thuthmosis III (1504– 1450 BC). The document in which the reports appear was found among the papers of the late Professor Tulli, the Egyptologist. Translated by Boris de Rachewitz the extract reads:

'In the year 22 third month of winter, sixth hour of day . . . the scribes of the House of Life found it was a circle of fire that was coming in the sky. (Though) it had no head, the breath of its mouth (had) a foul odour. Its body one rod (about 150 ft) long and one rod large. It had no voice. . . . Now after some days had passed over these things, Lo! they were more numerous than anything. They were shining in the sky to the limits of . . . heaven. . . . Powerful was the position of the fire circles. The army of the King looked on and His Majesty was in the midst of it. It was after supper. Thereupon, they (the fire circles) went up higher directed towards the South.'

The dragon as a fiery circle can be seen in early illustrations from China and the East, and a rock carving in Algonkin territory of Illinois was found to show a rampaging dragon inside a circle formed by his own tail.

As today flying saucers are both a portent and a part of great events to come, so in the earliest times their appearance gave warning of and led to the first great crisis in the history of the human race, the arrival of the gods on earth. Chinese dragon myths describe how the first flying saucers appeared to men. They were fiery or luminous. People were frightened by the shaft of light which they threw on to the earth by night. They flew without wings and landed on four legs on hilltops or in pits which later filled with water and became sacred ponds. They frequented mountains and high places, but were also associated with the sea, lakes and deep water. All these features are characteristic of modern flying saucer reports, and have been associated with unidentified flying objects throughout history. The shaft of light which illuminated the earth in the year before the landing of Cortez in Mexico was interpreted by astrologers to mean that the gods were about to return. This was why Montezuma hesitated to oppose the Spanish invaders; he took them for the gods and was anxious to do nothing to give them offence. The fire from the Spaniards' guns confirmed his belief that he was dealing not with men but with gods. Like the Tuatha De Danaan of Ireland who arrived from the air with fire and thunder, the gods are associated with flames in the sky. Their vehicles, the shining disc or fiery dragon have always terrified men and been seen as a portent of strange, supernatural events or of some change in the existing order.

When the luminous discs came down to earth they were seen to be the vehicles of a strange race of intelligent beings. For the first time in the history of the world men were confronted with something quite outside their terrestrial experience. Suddenly their minds became aware of things of which they had no previous conception, for it was only through contact with the gods that men first realised the possibility of a higher way of life. They imitated the gods in their own particular sciences. It was the serpent who introduced the knowledge on which our communal life depends, the use of fire and the arts of agriculture and medicine. We naturally think that our path to civilisation was the only one possible simply because our experience is limited to that which we received. Our entire perception is conditioned by knowledge of our own past. But it is based merely upon an almost forgotten encounter at the dawn of history with an extra-terrestrial form of life which may, for all we know, be only one degree superior to ourselves. The lessons we learnt, those which survived, have been developed up to the present state where no further advance is possible inside the existing system, but the scope for revolutionary development is infinite. Given one more key, another inspiration from outside, we may be capable of an expansion of consciousness comparable to that achieved as on the first occasion when we were visited by people from space.

The war between men and gods, the killing of the dragon, the expulsion of the serpent, all these myths refer to the times preceding the withdrawal from earth of the superior race. The tragedy which the sudden awareness of a higher potential brought to the human race is told in the Prometheus myth and that of the Garden of Eden. Prometheus, as Zeus knew, was no benefactor to mankind. The secrets he revealed, those which the serpent gave to Adam and Eve, were far beyond man's power to accept. The familiar tragedy of the impact of an advanced culture on a primitive race destroyed the equanimity of the human spirit. Men could use the gods' artefacts and instruments but knew nothing of the culture which underlay their possession. From this came war, the repeated decimation of the human race and the eventual acceptance by the gods that their presence on earth could cause nothing but continual strife. They withdrew and left men to sort out their affairs as best they could. It was left to a few men, the heroes who had known the gods, to maintain the system they had established. For some time these men, like the Romanised Britons after the withdrawal of the legions, tried to carry on the traditions of the gods. But since the imposed culture had never taken root among men, decay quickly set in. Knowledge atrophied, and those civilised customs which were still observed became mechanical rites, the reasons for whose continued practice were forgotten. Gradually the memory of the gods and their civilisation became confined to small groups of people in widely separated parts of the earth. Wherever the influence of these people was not felt, whole sections of the human race began to relapse into the state of nature in which they had been found. This process of degeneration continued into modern times, reaching its nadir in races such as the Tasmanians who by the middle of the nineteenth century, when they were finally exterminated, had almost returned to the primeval state, and the Andaman Islanders, a people so regressed that they had even lost the art of making fire. It was only a tradition of the gods and a vestigial memory of their secrets, preserved by certain sects and religious societies, that enabled our present form of civilisation to arise from the embers of the culture once established on earth by an extra-terrestrial race.

CHAPTER THREE

The Terrestrial History of Flight

The most dramatic achievement of early men in their imitation of the gods was the acquisition of the art of flying. Even during the decline which followed the gods' departure, this was a secret never entirely lost. The terrestrial history of aviation begins and ends with fact; in between is a vast period of memory, legend and anticipation. During the whole of that period the tradition of flight somehow kept alive, surviving the Middle Ages, when so much else was lost, simply through the curiosity of a few ecclesiastics, and finally re-emerging to make possible the partial rediscovery of the art in the twentieth century.

Even so, the lessons preserved from the past have only half been understood. Flight in prehistoric times was not achieved by engines, but by some natural force we have not yet rediscovered. The behaviour of the mysterious flying discs now seen all over the world, their acceleration, manœuvrability and enigmatic appearances, has led many to suggest that these objects use some element of which we are not yet aware or move along certain natural lines of force still undefined. If these flying saucers are in fact vehicles of extra-terrestrial origin, it is obvious that they use a means of propulsion of which we are absolutely ignorant. They move so quickly and change direction with such ease, they must use, or even be part of, some great natural current, electro-magnetic fields of force or some such invisible element. There is a tradition of which we can find tantalising fragments in early history and folklore, that the natural force used may have something to do with the power of sound.

This belief that sound can cause levitation is old and universal. It has been taken up and considerably developed by Theosophist writers, who have used their own methods to test it. A. P. Sinnett in *Stonehenge and the Pyramids* sets out to show that the stones of these and other great monuments of antiquity were levitated into position by the power of sound. He points out that the stones of the Pyramids fit together so nicely that, as Petrie said, 'a card could not be inserted between their joints', and this is an achievement that no modern contractor would care to attempt. The same could be said of the stone platform at Baalbek, hardly possible to reproduce even with the most powerful modern equipment, and of the mountain-top cities of Peru, built of stone blocks so huge that on a recent army exercise it was found impossible to raise them up the mountain from their quarries below. Sinnett claimed that a study of early documents and legends, confirmed by the occult methods of the Theosophists, revealed that there was a secret way in which stone could be levitated by sonic power. Professor Homet, the archæologist, quotes some fragments of these legends in his book *On the Trail of the Sun Gods*.

' "In ancient times" according to the folklore of Galway (in Ireland) "everyone danced in the air like leaves on the autumn wind. People could fly when they sung a certain refrain and clashed their cymbals."

"They (the priests) placed under the stones some papyri on which secret things were written, and then struck the stones with a wand . . . whereupon they were lifted into the air and came to the pyramids."

"In ancient times", say the verses of the Dzyan, "man could fly when he sang a certain refrain and clashed a cymbal."

The Dzyan is a Hebrew poem translated from ancient Sanscrit after having been written in old Chinese. Originally it was taken "from an ancient language which even in those remote times had already disappeared." '

Another form of the belief that sound can move stone occurs in the fairy stories where at the phrase 'open sesame' or some such formula a stone rolls away to reveal a treasure cave. British legends tell how Merlin transported the stones of Stonehenge over the sea from Ireland by magic, perhaps by a spoken spell, and there is even a reference to what might have been a stone flying machine. Mog Ruith, a powerful Druid, and his daughter Tlachtga, were pupils of Simon Magus, the witch whom St Peter caused to crash to the ground as he was demonstrating his powers of flight before the Roman emperor. The flying machine which Simon used was smashed by the fall and Tlachtga brought a piece of it back to Ireland and set it up near Tipperary where it is now known as the rock of Cleghele.

In many parts of the world are stories of vessels propelled by the power of sound. One of the versions of Cinderella has her going to the ball in a basket in which she sits singing, and a fairy princess who flew through the air on her bed levitated by her song is the heroine of the Indian fairy tale quoted by Mark Thornhill, *The Perfumier's Daughter*. Finnish mythology concerned with the hero, Wainamoinen, says that like Arthur he did not die, but departed to the west in a copper vessel which moved as he sang songs. A popular tale among the Bantus of Malawi told by Alice Werner in *Myths and Legends of the Bantu* has a similar theme.

A pretty young girl lived in a village with her parents. She had plenty of suitors, but always turned them down as not good enough for her. One day a stranger came into the village and the girl declared that he was the one man she fancied. Her parents were against the match as they knew nothing at all about the young man, but she insisted and finally had her way.

For some time after the marriage the couple lived happily together, then one day the man said he wanted to take his bride to visit his people in his own village. They left on the journey followed by the girl's little brother who would not leave them, though the girl said he was not nearly smart enough for her husband's people.

When they arrived at the village they were well received and given a fine hut to themselves. The boy however slept outside and at night saw a terrible thing. All the villagers, including his sister's husband, became hyenas and prowled around the girl's hut planning how they would eat her. Next day the boy told his sister and she sat up the following night to see for herself. When she saw the hyenas she was terrified and begged her brother to help her escape. This he promised to do. He went out into the forest at daybreak, cut down a tree and hollowed out the trunk. He sat in it, sang a song and the wooden vehicle floated up into the air, coming down in the centre of the village. The hyena-villagers were delighted, and asked him to show them how it was done. The boy signalled to his sister to stand near the craft, then he sat in it again and sung his song,

'Chinguli-changa, delu-delu.'

As he rose into the air his sister sprang in beside him, and they sailed up over the trees, leaving the hyenas screaming behind them.

43

When they arrived back at their village the girl was told that as a punishment for her stupidity she would never be allowed to marry again.

The Bantus are fond of this story and have several versions: in one of them the girl and her brother escape from peril by riding on a drum which flies when beaten. Exactly the same idea occurs in the Algonkin 'Swan-maiden' myth quoted in a later chapter, where the girl from the sky flies in a circular vessel, which rises when she sings a certain song.

The association of sound with levitation is repeated in the legends which tell of the great golden disc in the chief temple of the Incas. This was not made by them, but had been handed down from an older civilisation which had known the art of flying, and was guarded together with other secrets from the past by an initiated order of priests. Some say it was thrown into a lake when the Spanish came, or that it was melted down unknowingly as loot, and others claim that it is still kept in a secret centre of arcane knowledge deep in the Andes. The secret of the disc was that, when struck, the vibrations it set up caused levitation, and enabled its owner to fly through the air.

In recent times an experiment with sound as a motive force was carried out by a Philadelphian, John Keely, described by the Dictionary of American Biography as an 'inventor and impostor'. Keely gave up his career as the leader of an orchestra to make an engine driven by sound, as he put it by the 'intermolecular vibrations of ether'. In 1874 he claimed success. His machine, controlled by a note on the violin, attracted considerable attention. Unfortunately either through a certain lack of openness in his character or through the machinations of vested interests, something which such an invention was bound to attract and which has certainly caused the suppression of a great many inventions, particularly those which threatened the profits of the oil companies, Keely lost most of his financial support. Hounded by creditors and constantly threatened by prosecutions for fraud, he died penniless in 1898, and of his invention nothing more was heard.

The force which Keely may have rediscovered, or something like it, appears to have been known in the past. There are definite signs of it in the East, particularly in India, where records from extreme antiquity have been preserved in monasteries and temples. It was there that Colonel Churchward claimed to have found plans of a flying machine among ancient temple documents; also in Tibet arte-facts have been found whose purpose has not been guessed, but which some say to be machines for contacting some natural force which could provide a motive for levitation.

More certain is the fact that in India and China legends and historical documents show that at one time a form of flight was known, but was in a decadent stage, merely a memory of how it had been in the past. The notion of flight was inherited from the days of the gods, whose memory inspired men to seek to regain the art of levitation. The tradition of flying gods survived. Vishnu in post-Vedic literature had as his vehicle Garuda, the great bird; the supreme Vedic god, Indra, rode through the air in a golden chariot, in which he is frequently illustrated, riding inside this disc-shaped vehicle. Eastern mythology contains many references to the gods' flying discs, and other, larger objects appeared in the skies described in the legends of great mounds that flew around like birds and caused great damage when they landed on earth.

Men were never able to fly until they had learnt the art from the gods. One who was instructed by them was the emperor Shun of China (2258–08 BC). He may have lived at the very end of the gods' stay on earth, for he seems to have been trained to take over the government when the superior race departed. For some reason, maybe because of his friendship with the race of gods, Shun was dis-liked by his father and stepmother, who subjected him to endless persecution, although he himself behaved to them in a dutiful and correct manner. However, the two daughters of the god-emperor Yao had taught Shun to fly, and this enabled him to avoid the various attempts made on his life. On one occasion he was trapped by his parents on top of a tower, which they had set alight, but he was able to escape by flying down in the form of a dragon, the usual way of describing the use of a flying machine. As someone who was com-pletely loyal to the superior race, Shun never abused the knowledge he had been given; in fact he only flew when he had to. As the gods prepared to depart, Shun was given a share in the government and married the two girls, his flying instructors. When Yao's reign was over, Shun became emperor, and perhaps due to his flying ability was able to rule well and peacefully until his death.

Other men to whom the secret of flight was revealed did not behave as well as Shun. Bellerophon, for instance, given the flying machine called poetically the horse Pegasus, became arrogant and tried to fly up to the seat of the gods on Mount Olympus, an act which led to him being cast down to earth.

The use of the horse as homologue for a flying machine was common in India. Among the stories from 'The Thirty-two Tales of the Lions-Throne' quoted, as are many of these examples, by Berthold Laufer in his work, *The Prehistory of Aviation*, is one which describes how a craftsman appeared at a certain King's court leading a wooden horse which contained a mechanism to enable it to fly. The King bought the machine and the craftsman showed him the switch to press in order to make it rise. Unfortunately he did not show him how to descend and the King flew a very long way before he found the right switch and landed in a forest. After this he became a skilful flier, and piloted the machine back to the palace together with a girl he had met on his journey. The same sort of story occurs also in the Arabian Nights.

In China the more usual poetic image for a flying machine, the dragon, is used, but sometimes the horse appears as well. A composite creature, half horse, half dragon, was used by the god-emperor Huang Ti in his departure from earth. He sat on its back with his wife and ministers, about seventy people in all, and flew up into the sky. Minor officials, perhaps human beings who had fraternised with the god-race and were frightened of their own people's revenge should they be left behind, tried to cling on to strands of the dragon's beard, but these snapped off and hurled them on to the ground.

One of the obvious uses for an aeroplane is of course in war. The gods had used their flying ability to control men and put down revolt or dangerous behaviour. Several times the human race was on the point of being exterminated, and only a change of heart by one of the gods spared a few survivors. This is what lies behind the various myths of the flood and other cataclysms. In the Egyptian version a renegade god, Set, leads men in rebellion against the supreme Osiris. Horus is dispatched to deal with the trouble. In or in the shape of a disc he comes to earth, defeats Set and makes such a slaughter of his followers that the earth is running with blood. Only at the last minute is he prevented from completing his destruction.

As the secrets of the gods, whether freely given or acquired by theft or imitation, came into the possession of men, a number of communities must have arisen where technological knowledge had far outgrown basic culture. The cities of Sodom and Gomorrah may have been examples of this. Their destruction by a rain of brimstone from the air which Professor Agrest sees as the destruction of a huge store of rocket fuel by the departing gods, is more likely to have been the extermination of a decadent community by the gods whose secrets had been stolen and misused. The decadence of the men of Sodom and Gomorrah, typified by their hysterically homosexual behaviour towards Lot's extra-terrestrial visitors, may have led them into a state of destructive madness. This together with their technological knowledge could have made them so dangerous to the balance of nature and to the very existence of life on earth that they had to be destroyed.

Many Indian accounts exist of air battles between the gods, sometimes with the participation of their human pupils. Even those who deny that these accounts have any basis in fact must admit that the Indians some two thousand years ago treated them as historical descriptions and tried to recreate the flying machines. There was even possibly a surviving tradition of how to fly, a secret possessed only by a small guild of craftsmen. It was one of these who made the airship described in a story from the Panchatantra.

This craftsman had a friend, a weaver, who had ideas about marrying the King's daughter. To this end he made a plan. He persuaded his friend to make him a flying machine, such as the god Vishnu used. When the machine was ready, the weaver dressed himself in the costume of Vishnu, and flew up to the tower where the princess lived. Seeing, as she thought, the god Vishnu paying her court, the princess let the weaver into her room and they consummated a marriage of mutual consent. The King eventually discovered that his daughter had a lover, but, impressed when he learnt his identity, he started involving himself in all sorts of wild adventures, confident that his celestial son-in-law would extricate him if necessary. His mad behaviour led to all the neighbouring kings joining together to meet him in battle. In terror the King called on the weaver to help him. The poor weaver appeared over the battlefield on his airship, though he knew that his assistance would be of little use and he would inevitably be exposed. But the real Vishnu, jealous for his reputation, entered into the weaver's body and scattered the enemy.

There are a number of historical accounts of flying warriors in

India including Abhaya Kara, a ninth-century saint from Bengal who routed a Turkish army from an airship. A similar story was told to Stanley the African explorer when he was in Uganda. He includes it in his book *Through the Dark Continent*:

'One of the heroes of Nakivingi was a warrior named Kibaga, who possessed the power of flying. When the King warred with the Wanyoro, he sent Kibaga into the air to ascertain the whereabouts of the foe, who, when discovered by this extraordinary being, were attacked on land in their hiding-places by Nakivingi, and from above by the active and faithful Kibaga, who showered great rocks on them and by these means slew a vast number. It happened that among the captives of Unyoro Kibaga saw a beautiful woman, who was solicited by the King in marriage. As Nakivingi was greatly indebted to Kibaga for his unique services, he gave her to Kibaga as wife, with a warning, however, not to impart the knowledge of his power to her, lest she should betray him. For a long time after the marriage his wife knew nothing of his power, but suspecting something strange in him from his repeated sudden absences and reappearances at his home, she set herself to watch him, and one morning as he left his hut, she was surprised to see him suddenly mount into the air with a burden of rocks slung on his back. On seeing this she remembered the Wanyoro complaining that more of their people were killed by some means from above than from the spears of Nakivingi, and Delilah-like, loving her race and her people more than she loved her husband, she hastened to her people's camp, and communicated, to the surprise of the Wanyoro, what she had that day learned. To avenge themselves on Kibaga, the Wanyoro set archers in ambush on the summits of each lofty hill, with instructions to confine themselves to watching the air and listening for the brushing of his wings, and to shoot their arrows in the direction of the sound, whether anything was seen or not. By this means on a certain day, as Nakivingi marched to the battle, Kibaga was wounded to the death by an arrow, and upon the road large drops of blood were seen falling, and on coming to a tall tree the King detected a dead body entangled in its branches. When the tree was cut down Nakivingi saw that it was the body of his faithful warrior Kibaga.'

Among the Indians the secret of making airships was said to be the property of a guild of Greek craftsmen, perhaps a colony of expatriates who had somehow become the heirs to the tradition or had rediscovered it from the study of old documents. A seventeenth-century Sanscrit romance tells how King Kakavarna wanted to go up in an airship. The only man who knew how to make one was a Greek prisoner. This man constructed the airship and the King set off on a flight from which he never returned. Another Indian story is of how a certain Vicvila made friends with some Greek craftsmen and learnt from them how to fly. He made an airship, described as a mechanical cock, and went for a trip through the air. The King sent for him to find out the secret of his vehicle, but Vicvila refused to give it on the grounds that it was something which no one must reveal and was only known to Greeks. Vicvila's father-in-law happened to be a carpenter and the King thought he might have had something to do with the building of the airship. He told him that unless he revealed the secret it would be the worse for him. The father-in-law therefore begged Vicvila to tell him the secret and save his life, but Vicvila refused to do so and instead, when night had fallen, he and his wife mounted the flying machine and escaped together to a far country.

The King then ordered his native craftsmen to make him an airship. They were in despair until a stranger appeared who claimed that he knew the secret and offered to help. Materials were provided for him and one of the craftsmen ventured to suggest that he might first enquire of the King how many people he intended taking on the flight. It has been known in the past, he said, for a flying contrivance to be made and then be unable to leave the ground because of the number of passengers. The stranger was scornful of this suggestion. The people who made such vehicles, he said, must have been ignorant provincials. His machine would carry any number. In fact, when it was ready, a considerable number of people did climb on to the airship: the King, his wife, his harem, ministers, and representatives from each urban corporation. They set off on a long and delightful voyage, stopping occasionally for sight-seeing or for the King to perform his religious duties at sacred centres.

Among the reasons given by Vicvila for not revealing his secret was the apparently whimsical one that the art of making flying machines was only of interest because very few people knew how to do it. If it became common knowledge it would enjoy no more prestige than the manufacture of beds. If everyone knew how to fly, it would be no more fun for those few who now possessed the secret. In this statement can be found one of the reasons why flying eventually became a lost art. After the departure of the gods, the general level of culture declined to a point where much of the knowledge and skills which the gods had introduced died out, either because there was no further use and application for them or because no one bothered to learn them. The proper construction of a flying machine, such as the gods made with their human apprentices, must have been a complicated matter demanding experts in several different crafts and materials from remote and widely separated areas. With the decline of human society into small and mutually hostile communities the construction of elaborate airships was no longer possible. However the theory was preserved by certain religious groups and communities and eventually came to form part of the records of the great organised religious houses of the East. From time to time documents were studied and a primitive form of flight recreated. This may be how the Greek community came by the secret. To the people of their own time it was just a toy, an expensive and entertaining gadget suitable for kings to play with but quite outside the reach of the common people. A further reason for its suppression is given in a story from a Chinese history book of the third century.

'Ki-Kung-Shi was able to make a flying chariot which driven by a fair wind travelled a great distance. At the time of the emperor Ch'ing T'ang (1766–54 BC, founder of the Shang Dynasty) the west wind blew Ki-Kung's chariot as far as Yu-chou. The emperor ordered this chariot to be destroyed that it should not become known to the people. Ten years later when the east wind blew, the emperor ordered another chariot of this kind to be built by Ki-Kung and sent him back in it.'

Although the word here used for a flying chariot is apparently the same as that in modern China for an aeroplane, it seems probable that Ki-Kung flew in a sort of glider, or balloon. But the fact that the emperor had the vehicle destroyed shows what little future there was for aviation under a feudal system. If the knowledge of it was acquired by the common people, no fortress and no throne would be safe. Any attempt to re-introduce flight was therefore stamped out.

The legendary skill of Greek craftsmen in manufacturing flying machines does not seem to be recorded in their native histories, although theatrical machines, in which people appeared to descend from the sky, were used on the stage, and the concept of flight was kept alive in stories such as that of Daedalus and Icarus. It may have been their inspiration which led to one of the first strictly historical accounts of the construction of a flying machine. It was built by a Pythagorean philosopher and mathematician, Archytas (428–347 BC), a Greek living in southern Italy. The machine was driven by a system of weights and by compressed air, and worked for some time until its inventor was drowned in the Adriatic. Archytas was the first of the great number of men in Europe who experimented with flight all through the historical period. Since his time many attempts at aviation were made, some highly ingenious and all of great interest since they show how the idea of flight persisted. All through the Middle Ages optimistic inventors, equipped with wings and devices of all sorts, launched themselves from towers, a form of experiment which, if unsuccessful, tended to preclude the possibility of any further attempts by the same man. Another deterrent to flyers was the attitude of the Church. Early systems of religion, replaced by Christianity, looked to the sky for their gods, and had strong traditions of people from the sky coming to earth and of flying men. It is possible that in Europe as well as in the East a certain knowledge of flight survived in organised religious establishments. The Druids were said to know and to practise the art. One who made use of their knowledge was King Bladud, father of King Lear, who was killed in 852 BC when his airship crashed on to the temple of Apollo in London. The knowledge that their predecessors had worshipped flying beings and even practised levitation themselves led the early Christians to attribute all manifestations of flight to diabolic power. As far as possible all documents relating to it were destroyed and traditions suppressed. Anyone who experimented with flight was suspected and persecuted. Yet as a result of their obsession with the subject, such knowledge of flight as survived became the property of Christian monks and scholars, and some of them were even allowed to conduct experiments with it. The Franciscan Roger Bacon, who was acquainted with ancient works on aviation, mostly now lost, wrote extensively on the subject. The monk Oliver of Malmesbury in about

1020 injured himself during a partly successful attempt to fly from the top of a tower. John Damion, abbot of Tungland in 1507, flew from the top of Stirling Castle but fell breaking his bones. These men because of their privileged position inside the Church were able to make their experiments with impunity. Others were less fortunate. Father Laurenco de Gusmao at the end of the seventeenth century made and flew a sort of glider and experimented with a hot air balloon which during a performance at the Royal Palace in Lisbon set fire to the curtains. Gusmao was persecuted by the Inquisition and had to leave Portugal.

Although the centres of learning established under previous religious systems were destroyed by the early Christians, who did however, as later in Mexico, become the heirs of a certain amount of their scholarship, some vestiges of the old system survived in places all over Europe. Dr Margaret Murray and others have seen in the witch cults of western Europe a persistence of the pre-Christian religious tradition, a degenerate form, growing ever weaker through persecution and lack of central organisation, of an extremely old system of knowledge and worship. Within the witch cult may have survived the last feeble memory of the art of levitation. It is well known that witches claimed to fly. Even though to confess as much usually led to their execution, witches still boasted of their flying powers. One of the Salem witches burned in 1682 said that she had become lame through falling off her broomstick on her way to a meeting; the seventeen Pendle witches sentenced to death in 1633, but pardoned by the enlightened Charles I, were said to have flown over the river Ribble together with their familiars; Julian Cox was executed as a witch in Taunton for having flown in the air. Isobel Gowdie, a seventeenth-century Scottish witch, made a beautiful confession of her experiences in flight:

'I had a little horse, and would say, "HORSE AND HATTOCK IN THE DEVIL'S NAME!" And then we would fly away where we would be, even as straws would fly upon a highway. We will fly like straws when we please; wild-straws and corn-straws will be horses to us, and we put them betwixt our foot and say, "HORSE AND HATTOCK IN THE DEVIL'S NAME!" And when any sees these straws in a whirlwind and does not sanctify themselves, we may shoot them dead at our pleasure. Any that are shot by us, their soul will go to heaven, but their bodies remain with us, and will fly as horses to us, as small as straws.'

Some say that witches merely received the sensation of flight through the use of belladonna, aconite and other drugs. But there is nothing extraordinary or unusual in obsessed and ecstatic people achieving levitation, and, from what we know of them through their behaviour at their trials, witches enjoyed a detached, elevated or hysterical state of mind rarely found outside magic or religion. This state, achieved by starvation, isolation and prayer or in other ways familiar to mystics, has been experienced inside most religions. The list of Christian saints and ascetics who were prone to levitation is a long one. The Rev. Montague Summers gives some examples: St Francis of Assisi, St Catherine of Siena, St Colette, Raimiero di Borgo San-Sepulchro, St Catherine de Ricci, St Alphonsus Rodriguez S.J., St Mary Magdalen de Pazzi, Raimond Rocco, Bl. Charles de Sezze, St Veronica Guiliani, St Gerard Majella, Anne Catherine Emmerich, Dominca Barbagli, the ecstatica of Montesanto-Savino who levitated daily, St Ignatius Loyola, St Theresa and St John of the Cross, St Alphonsus Liguori who rose several feet above the ground while preaching to a large congregation, Gemma Galgani of Lucca in 1901, and, best known of all, St Joseph of Cupertino whose spectacular levitations were such an embarrassment to himself and his fellow Capuchins that he was sent to a remote monastery, where he would cause less distraction, and only permitted to say Mass at a private altar.

As the memory of the old gods gradually faded, the culture they had left behind ceased to develop, and the knowledge on which it was founded became atrophied, surviving only in tribal ritual or, at best, among the members of closed religious castes such as the Druids. In the West the resulting intellectual void was filled by Christianity, a system fundamentally different from those it supplanted in that it is more concerned in practice with social and moral issues than with the nature of God and the interpretation of the universal pattern, questions with which earlier, non-Christian religions were wholly obsessed. Christianity, inaugurated and inspired by the appearance of the Son of God on earth, was far more urgent and vital than the old religions, the physical appearance of whose gods was by then a matter merely of tradition. The new religion, although uniquely strong in its possession of a recently manifest god, did not destroy all memory of the old. In fact it had to incorporate it in its own system to such an extent that, as is often observed, the only original figure in Christianity is that of Christ himself. Every other theme derives from a much older mythology. The flying gods of former times were christianised into angels and cherubim, and in any other form their worship or even any mention of them was suppressed. Only Christian scholars had easy access to documents and records describing flight in the past, and in course of time it came generally to be believed that nothing of the sort had ever been known; that flying people were mythical in the sense that they had never really existed. In the same way as, having for many centuries persecuted and murdered witches, the Church was later able to declare that it did not believe in them, that there was no such thing, so in the course of time even Christian priests forgot about the flying beings whose memory they had once so keenly suppressed. Even when faced with the firmest evidence to the contrary they could not believe that flight was actually practised. Agobard, a ninth-century Bishop of Lyons, provided an example of this disbelief. He was told that the people of Lyons were lynching some peasants who had suddenly landed in the middle of the city from out of the sky. The Bishop intervened and saved the men because, he said, the story of what had happened was too ridiculous to be believed. Their story was indeed strange. They had been working in the fields when some objects came down from the sky and landed nearby. Men appeared and forced the peasants to enter these objects. The next thing they knew they were being set down in the middle of Lyons. It was fortunate for them that the dangerous tradition of flight in pre-Christian times had by then been suppressed.

The incident is only one of the many recorded from the Middle Ages which must have helped to revive the idea of flight in people's minds. Recent interest in the subject has led writers like Harold Wilkins and W. R. Drake to examine early reports and reassess them in the light of the post-war saucer experience. Jacques Vallée in his study of the evidence for flying saucers, 'Anatomy of a Phenomenon', comments,

'We have on file more than three hundred UFO sightings prior to the twentieth century and, although it is difficult to comment upon them in the light of scientific analysis, we feel they should be treated exactly as modern reports in respect of their psychological and sociological aspects.'

It is always hard to assess the importance of reports from another age, particularly those originally based on hearsay rather than on first-hand experience. For example there is the remarkable story about the appearance of an airship over the church at Gravesend, Kent. It appears in several books of Irish legends and also in the works of Gervase of Tilbury, a twelfth-century monk who collected many of the legends and beliefs of his time. As he tells it, the airship appeared as people were leaving the church after Mass. An anchor was thrown down on a rope and a man slid down it into the churchyard, but as people gathered round him it was seen that he was unable to breathe and he soon died 'stifled in our gross air, as a shipwrecked mariner would be in the sea'. At this the airship flew away, leaving behind the anchor, which was later made into hoops for the church door.

This story may be hard to accept as it stands, but there are others more direct and better documented. Leslie quotes from a manuscript found at Ampleforth in 1953 which describes a flying saucer being seen over Byland Abbey, Yorkshire, in January 1290. It has been translated as:

'Took the sheep from Wilfred and roasted them on the feast of SS. Simon and Jude. But when Henry the abbot was about to say grace, John, one of the brethren, came in and said there was a great portent outside. Then they all ran out and Lo! a large round silver thing like a disc (res grandis, circumcircularis argentea, disco quondam haud dissimilis) flew slowly over them and excited the greatest terror.'

Another much quoted passage from *Historia Anglorum* of Matthew of Paris describes how on 1 January 1254 at St Alban's Abbey at midnight 'a large kind of ship, elegantly shaped, well equipped and of a marvellous colour' passed in the sky over the heads of the monks who watched it by the light of the moon and stars. Two hundred years later a similar sight was observed over Arras in France. On this occasion fire was seen to issue from the vessel. Fire was also associated with the objects in the sky recorded in the Anglo-Saxon Chronicle of 793 AD:

'In this year terrible portents appeared over Northumbria and miserably frightened the inhabitants, these were exceptional flashes of lightning and fiery dragons were seen flying in the air.'

This would seem to be an unmistakable reference to flying saucers described in the conventional way as dragons. It is by no means unique. Contemporary documents throughout the Middle Ages and earlier give instances of moving lights in the sky, circular objects, men in airships and similar phenomena, usually treated as portents of some earthly events. Reports such as these kept the notion of flight alive in people's minds. Together with the traditions of flight in the past they inspired continual attempts to recapture the art of flying, and led to its partial rediscovery in the early part of this century. The appearance of flying saucers however has made it clear that the knowledge of flight which we have attained is based on terrestrial concepts and contains no advance towards the revelation of that natural force by which flight was achieved on earth in the past.

CHAPTER FOUR

Another Race on Earth

The most interesting aspect of the modern flying saucer legend is the general assumption that these objects are extra-terrestrial space craft containing beings from another part of the universe. Reports and rumours of contact with their occupants has led to a revival of the old belief in the other race, a people who, although having much the same physical existence as ourselves, are unlike us in their nature and origin. A tradition of these people, surviving from the days when, as a superior race of gods, they appeared openly on earth, has everywhere continued up to the present time, refreshed by the occasional reappearance of certain of their members, and now assuming a more definite form in our increasing interest in the possibility of extra-terrestrial life.

In the past, when any conception of this possibility hardly existed, and would in any case have been considered heretical, the supernatural race was divided into certain categories – fairies, demons and the like – whose nature was variously defined but whose origin was only vaguely understood.

Shakespeare is generally considered to be the first writer to describe fairies in their later form as unsubstantial, picturesque creatures, the descendants of the spirits of nature, equipped with tiny wings, shy but friendly. In this character fairies are hardly comparable with the beings who feature in modern flying saucer reports. But the true fairy tradition, one which has persisted on a popular level up to this century, describes fairies as creatures very much like ourselves, only rather smaller. Their existence was undoubted, but since their origins were suspect, it was considered wise to keep out of their way, and anyone who had dealings with them was liable to be persecuted. Up to the seventeenth century people were brought to trial for mixing with the fairy race, and in the records of their trials several contemporary accounts of fairies have survived. In all cases they appear to look so much the same as ordinary people. A north country woman, Bessie Dunlop, actually took a fairy lover called Tom Reid, and through him met the Queen of Elfland, a stout woman who visited her when she was in bed for the birth of her baby. The Queen was also described at the trial of Isobel Gowdie. She was 'brawly clothed in white linens and in white and brown clothes'. Her husband the King was 'a braw man well favoured and broad-faced'. Isobel Gowdie visited them in the hillock where they lived and also saw some tiny bulls who, she said, were 'routing and skoylling up and down there and affrightened me'.

Although similar to men in appearance, fairies were of a different order of existence to the human race. This is illustrated in the Irish story of the priest, riding home one evening, who saw a little man by the side of the road. The man said he had an important question to ask him, whether there was any mention in the Bible of the possibility of Redemption for the fairy people. The priest drew out his Bible and answered, 'There is only Redemption for those of the seed of Adam'. Whereupon from the bogs around arose the sound of all the fairies lamenting.

From this it is evident that fairies were of a different origin to men. But their peculiarly sinister character derived from their close similarity to ordinary people, which made it possible for them to infiltrate human communities without being detected.

In this they aroused the most deep-rooted of all fears, the suspicion that there may be people among us who are not of the same origin as ourselves. This fear, which has been behind all of the hysterical persecutions of foreigners and minorities throughout history, has recently become attached to the figures now associated with the flying saucers.

In a public lecture which he gave in April 1966, Dr John Cleary Baker expressed in modern terms an old and widely held belief. There are those among us, he said, who although of ordinary human appearance are actually motivated by some extra-terrestrial force. These people, among whom he claimed to have recognised some occupying important positions in society, are possessed of an alien spirit. It is as if an operation has been performed on their brains such as scientists say is now possible, whereby they act entirely in accordance with suggestions put out by some central agency. Dr Baker saw these people as in some way connected with the flying saucer phenomenon.

The theme of aliens being within human society is one which novelists have always found attractive. It occurs frequently in the works of Dostoievski, whose heroes, figures such as Stavrogin in 'The Devils' and 'The Idiot' Prince Mishkin, are inspired by alien spirits which sets them apart from other men. The influence of the recent flying saucer legend has revived our consciousness of the possibility that alien infiltrators may now be living among us. The idea has been extensively developed in science fiction and comics. The Soviet writer Sinyavski, now serving a prison sentence, published a short story in *Encounter* early in 1966 which described the arrival on earth of a being from another planet. An inter-planetary space craft from some remote centre of life crashed in the north Russian wilderness. The sole survivor was a creature of great intelligence, of quite inhuman appearance and function, but by studying the local tribes and finally mixing with them, he learnt about men and their customs and managed to adapt his shape into one passably human, that of a hunchback. He made his way to Moscow and lived there miserably but unobtrusively, preserving the secret of his identity by being able to avoid intimate human contact.

Whether or not something of the sort has ever actually happened is a question which we are not yet in a position to answer. Some years ago it would have received little serious attention. Recently, however, things have happened which have compelled us to look at past events in a new light, and to revalue certain historical phenomena, which have never hitherto been explained. Since the 1939–45 war three new influences have made themselves felt. First, the reports and rumours of flying saucers, which have led to the revival of old beliefs long dormant; secondly, many scientists now state their opinion that there is intelligent life outside the earth and even that certain forms of it have visited the earth in the past; thirdly the rise of a body of literature dealing, often in a revolutionary way, with the question of extra-terrestrial life. The fact that this form of writing started on a popular level, way down the literary scale, in comics, flying saucer books and space novels, indicates the wide basis of its appeal.

For these three reasons there is growing renewed interest in the possibility of alien beings on earth. The most popular form of speculation, that employed by Dr Baker, is that they may have come in the way to which our basic fears most respond, as spies infiltrating human society. The usual implication is that they are preparing the way for an invasion of the earth by their own people.

This sort of theory may seem over-fanciful, and it suffers from the obvious weakness that it imputes human ambitions for power to a race presumably superior and certainly different to ourselves. Nevertheless there is a number of reasons for suspecting that since the departure of the gods we have occasionally been visited by individual members of an alien race. From time to time creatures, in varying degrees human, have appeared inexplicably on earth in circumstances which make it hard to attribute to them any terrestrial origin.

Such a creature was reported in the eleventh century in Orford on the coast of Suffolk. The 'Merman of Orford' as he came to be called, was caught from the sea in some fishermen's nets and taken back to the port. Orford is now a village on a silted estuary, dominated by a towering castle. Hilaire Belloc wrote of his visit,

'*The men that lived in Orford stood*
Upon the shore to meet me;
Their faces were like carven wood,
They did not wish to greet me.'

At the time of the 'Merman's' appearance Orford was a prosperous port, but his impression of its inhabitants could have been no better than Belloc's. They walled him into a cell in the castle and interrogated him cruelly. Although, apart from his exceptionally hairy appearance, the 'Merman' looked like an ordinary man, he had evidently enjoyed no previous contact with the human race. He knew no human customs or language, ate only raw fish and, to the surprise of his captors, gave absolutely no sign of reverence when taken into the church. In an attempt to make him talk, the men of Orford put the 'Merman' to all kinds of torture, but nothing was ever learnt of who he was or where he was from. After some time in captivity he escaped to the sea. All attempts to recapture him were in vain, for he was an excellent swimmer and easily evaded his pursuers and their nets. But suddenly he gave up, returned to land and let himself be led back to the castle and locked up. Finally after more ill-treatment he escaped again, and this time did not return.

The 'Merman' was not the only mysterious being to appear in Suffolk in the eleventh century. Two remarkable looking children were found just outside the village of Woolpit in the west part of the county. They appeared to come from a crater in the ground. They also could speak no English, but the striking thing about them was their colour; they were green. The villagers were kind to the children, a little girl about twelve and her younger brother. They gave them food, but the children were unable to eat anything but beans. When they had learned to speak they said they came from a place called St Martins, but could not account for their sudden appearance in Woolpit. Their first impression had been the ringing of the church bells, the first sound they had heard. In the course of time the children lost their green colour and became quite human in appearance. The little boy died, but the girl survived, entered domestic service with a local gentleman and finally married a man from King's Lynn in Norfolk.

Judging by the impression they made on the people among whom they appeared, it is evident that neither the Orford 'merman' nor the green children of Woolpit were regarded as entirely human. Various suggestions have been made on what sort of creatures they really were. The 'merman' has been implausibly interpreted as a wanderer from some wild race such as the Eskimos or Finns or even as a sea-lion; some folklorists have seen in the green children the last survivors of an aboriginal race, the same as that which is said to have contributed to the legend of the fairies. It may be that like the wild Indian boy, the last of his tribe, who was found in the early years of this century near the west coast of America having spent his whole life without seeing anyone other than his family and knowing nothing of white civilisation, the children were the last representatives of an otherwise vanished race. But although a great deal of fairy lore does derive from memories and legends of a degenerate aboriginal people, there is more to it than that. First-hand accounts of meetings with fairies have continued up to this century, certainly to times sufficiently recent for any identifiable survival of a former race to be impossible and for any genuine memory of it to have vanished. If fairies are based on a memory of real people, it must be of a people who existed until very recently or who exist today. Not only are fairies of the traditional sort still occasionally reported, but their legend has recently been vividly revived in that of the flying saucers. In many cases the derided 'little green men' associated with flying saucers are described in exactly the same terms as were fairies in the past. If one can see flying saucers as the modern equivalent for the little boats, huts, fairy rings and glass towers in which fairies used to appear, the comparison is even closer.

The persistent vivid reports from all ages of fairies and supernatural creatures raises the inevitable question: what exactly is it that inspires the fairy legend? In a recent *Flying Saucer Review* Gordon Creighton made an interesting comment. 'There is much evidence', he wrote, 'that *some* of what we nowadays call "beings from flying saucers" are much more probably creatures who share this Earth with us; creatures who are totally unknown to most of us; regarding whom Science has not a single word to say; but about whom our own written and oral traditions, in all our civilisations, speak volumes'.

It is this conformity with the traditions of which Mr Creighton speaks that gives the creatures from flying saucers their peculiar significance.

In 1964 Jacques Vallée, a writer on the subject of flying saucers, made a survey for *Flying Saucer Review* of the cases where people had reported meetings with the occupants of these craft. In many of them the same phrases are used which might in the past have described fairies, gnomes and elves. 'A hairy dwarf', 'Two men and one woman, height 4½ feet, friendly, amber-coloured hair', and 'A midget, one metre thirteen, big shining yellow eyes, black face, shining green body'. In another flying saucer report, quoted by Aimé Michel in *Flying Saucers and the Straight Line Mystery*, appears the figure of what seems to be an elf or leprechaun.

'About dusk on 6 November 1957 John Trasco of Everittstown, New Jersey, went out to feed King, his six-year-old Belgian police dog, tethered at the side of the house. Mrs Trasco in the kitchen heard King bark furiously, and looked out to see a bright light in front of the barn, which is some sixty feet from the house, with shrubbery between. "I thought at first it was a puddle of water" (reflecting the sunset), she said. Then she realised that it was a luminous egg-shaped object, only three or four yards long, "just going up and down" a few feet off the ground, in front of the barn.'

Because of the shrubbery she did not see the 'little man' that her husband was confronting. The visitor was only 2½ or 3 feet tall, dressed in a 'green suit with shiny buttons, with a green hat like a tam, and gloves with a shiny object at the tip of each glove.' His face was putty-coloured, his nose and chin prominent, and his eyes large, protuberant, and frog-like. In a voice that was 'sharp and scary' he addressed Mr Trasco in 'broken language, as if he came from the other side' (i.e. from Europe). Mr Trasco thought he said, 'We are a peaceful people. We don't want no trouble. We just want your dog.'

Mr Trasco shouted at the little man and tried to grab him, but he jumped into his flying saucer and made off leaving some green powder on Mr Trasco's hands. The story ends farcically with Mrs Trasco telling a reporter, 'I told John we should have let them take King. He's half blind, and so cross I don't know who else would ever want him.'

The custom of fairies stealing animals and even people is well known. The only detail in the story of the little elf of Everittstown to distinguish it from earlier fairy stories is the appearance of the flying saucer in which the little man travelled. Earlier fairies were said to fly through the air in whirlwinds or in clouds of vapour or by using some means of levitation. Sometimes they sailed in fairy vessels. The remarkable encounter with two fairies in about 1910, which appears in Alasdair Alpin Macgregor's *The Peat-Fire Flame*, would certainly have been told in terms of a flying saucer contact had it occurred within the last twenty years. The story was told to Macgregor by Rev. Alexander Frazer, Minister of the Small Isles, who had it from the family concerned.

The encounter took place in the lonely island of Muck off the west coast of Scotland. The two sons of a local man, Sandy MacDonald, aged about ten and seven were playing on the beach when they found an unopened tin. As they were trying to open it, they saw a beautiful delicate looking little boy, a stranger to the island, standing beside them. He was dressed all in green. The boy invited them to come and look at his boat, and they saw a tiny vessel floating on the sea a few feet from the shore. A little girl three feet high and a dog about the size of a rat were in the boat, and the girl offered the children some tiny biscuits which they ate. After they had inspected the boat which was beautifully built with everything perfectly arranged, the green boy and girl said it was time for them to leave. They said goodbye to the two boys and told them, 'We will not be coming back here, but others of our race will be coming'.

Others may indeed have come, both as casual visitors and as

deliberate infiltrators into human communities. The green children of Woolpit seem to have been of the latter kind. This is one of several features which they have in common with the enigmatic figure of the Foundling of Nuremberg, Kaspar Hauser, whose history is by far the best documented of its kind, and may provide the key to the identity of other mysterious creatures of his sort.

Of all the mystery stories so popular in the nineteenth century none caused more sensation, misery and scandal than that of Kaspar Hauser. He was first seen on the outskirts of Nuremberg on Whit Monday, 28 May 1828. A cobbler standing outside his house noticed an odd looking youth eccentrically dressed tottering towards him as if hardly able to stand up. As he approached he held out a letter which the cobbler saw was addressed to the Captain of a cavalry regiment stationed in the town. The boy, who appeared to be about sixteen or seventeen years old could understand nothing said to him and repeated only one phrase, something like, 'I want to be a soldier like my father was'. A friend of the cobbler conducted the boy with great difficulty to the house of the captain to whom the letter was addressed. When they arrived, the boy, utterly exhausted and suffering dreadfully from blistered feet, sank down on some straw and went to sleep.

The captain came home some hours later and went to see the creature who had arrived at his house. They managed to wake him up and tried to question him, but he understood nothing and spoke only his one phrase. He was thereupon taken to the police station and put into a cell where he again slept. The letter he brought was examined. The anonymous writer asked for the boy to be allowed to become a soldier as his father had been. Together with this letter was another requesting the first writer to educate the child and send him into the cavalry when he was seventeen years old.

It soon became apparent that the boy was not an idiot as was first thought, but that his mind was as unawakened as a baby's, his senses undeveloped, and he had not the slightest idea of who or where he was nor of the meaning of anything he saw around him. He knew a few words including 'Ross', a dialect word for horse, and this inspired one of the policemen to give him a toy horse. He was delighted with the toy, seeming for the first time to break out of his mood of terrified stupor. He was next given a pencil and paper. These he seized and carefully wrote the words 'Kaspar Hauser', the name he

64

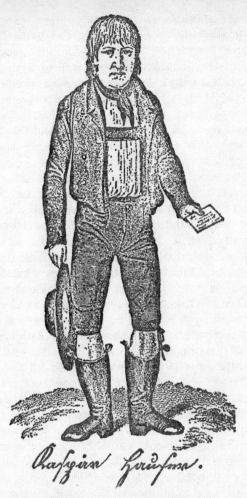

Fig. 2 The foundling of Nuremberg

was ever afterwards known by.

The news of the appearance of the strange boy created a sensation in Nuremberg. Crowds flocked to stare at him, question him and make experiments. It was apparent that he could eat and drink only bread and water. The mere presence of coffee, beer or strong drink in the same room caused him acute nausea, as did the sight of meat. A drop of brandy secretly mixed into this water made him sick. Various tricks such as this were tried out by his visitors. They waved swords at him to see if he would show signs of terror. They tried him for any religious feeling. But he was evidently quite strange to the world, suffering headaches from ordinary light, ignorant of the meaning of sounds, hardly able to use his hands and suffering dreadfully from blistered feet, as if he had never before walked in his life.

Some time after his arrival, a young scholar, Professor Daumer became interested in Kaspar Hauser, and undertook his education. He learnt quickly and very soon could speak enough to give an account of all he knew of his past existence.

It was an extraordinary story. All his life he had spent in a cell six or seven feet long, about four feet wide and six feet high. There were two small blocked up windows in the cell, but no light or sound of any kind ever penetrated from outside. Yet the cell was always of an even temperature, so that he was comfortable in just a shirt and trousers, and was dimly lit from some infallible source which was never apparent. Bread and water were always beside him when he woke up. Sometimes the water tasted funny and made him go to sleep. When this happened he found when he woke up that his nails had been cut and a clean shirt put on him. There was no day or night for him. He spent his time sitting against a wall with his legs stretched in front of him or playing with some toy horses which were the only things in the cell with him. Apart from himself and the toy horses, Kaspar Hauser had, at this time, no notion that there were any other creatures in the world. This existence was once interrupted. A hand reached from behind him, placed a board with a sheet of paper on his knees, gave him a pencil and guided his hand in tracing words and letters, including his name, Kaspar Hauser. He now had something else to occupy him apart from the horses, and spent hours writing on paper, copying out the words he had been shown.

The next event in his life was his release. He was lifted up, taken down some steps and in a dazed state was led for a long time until he and his unknown companion arrived at the spot where he first entered the human world. Here for the first time boots were put on to his feet, a letter thrust into his hand and his companion vanished.

Professor Daumer began an examination of his protégé and discovered some odd things about him. For a few days after his arrival Kaspar Hauser was distraught and unable to use his faculties. Then one morning he heard church bells and, soon, other sounds began to have a meaning for him. His hearing was abnormally acute, his eyesight even more so. He saw in the dark as well as by day, and in the twilight best of all. One dark evening he pointed out a gnat caught in a spider's web some considerable distance away, a sight invisible to anyone else until they had gone right up to the spot he indicated. His sense of smell was acute, causing him great suffering. Indeed for the first few weeks the new sensations he was constantly undergoing kept him in a state of sickness and misery, which only gradually subsided.

In other ways Kaspar Hauser's senses were unnaturally developed. He was sensitive to electricity. A magnet held towards him affected him peculiarly, the north pole in a different way to the south; he became an excellent rider partly through the attraction which his feet had for the iron of the stirrups; a thunderstorm – he had never heard thunder in his cell – caused him violent shuddering and pain. He was also able to distinguish between different metals by passing his hand over them even when they were covered by a cloth. Professor Daumer conducted several such experiments with him using gold, silver, brass and steel. Always he could detect their presence and tell one from the other. These powers and others of an equally phenomenal nature gradually declined as Kaspar Hauser grew more able to live as a normal human being. This was particularly so after he started to eat meat. At the same time he underwent a physical change. At the time of his arrival his features were noticeably brutish in character, his jaw prominent and his whole aspect in some way coarse and repulsive. An odd thing about him was that his knees were deformed, the slight hollow which is normal on the back of the legs opposite the knee-cap being in his case replaced by a lump, so that when he sat against a wall with his legs stretched out, every part of them touched the floor. This deformity remained all the rest of his life, but gradually his features improved. In a few months he grew into an intelligent refined looking boy, unrecognisable as the idiotic creature he appeared upon his arrival.

In October of the year following his appearance an attempt was made on Kaspar Hauser's life. A man, the same according to him as had taken him from his cell, entered the house of Professor Daumer when the family were out, struck the boy a blow with a knife and made off hurriedly, leaving him for dead. Fortunately the wound was not serious. The attack caused great concern in Nuremberg and re-awakened popular interest in the problem of their Foundling. Among those who heard the news was an Englishman travelling on the Continent, Lord Stanhope. He became interested in the story, went to Nuremberg and had an interview with Kaspar Hauser. As a result of this an intimate friendship grew up between the two of them, a friendship which later caused Lord Stanhope considerable embarrassment, and led eventually to bitter recriminations by the friends of Kaspar Hauser on the one hand and Lord Stanhope and his family on the other. In explaining the relationship between Kaspar Hauser and Lord Stanhope one can only say that Stanhope was doubtless rather a lonely man. His father, the son of the Prime Minister, Pitt, had been overbearing and terrifying to his family. He was both a clever inventor and a bully. On one occasion, having invented and had built a fire proof house, he compelled his guests to enter it while he set it on fire. His daughter, Lady Hester Stanhope, was another of his children who reacted against the father's authoritarian manner.

Whatever it was that attracted Lord Stanhope to Kaspar Hauser, the two became inseparable, driving out and dining in restaurants together, while Lord Stanhope, thinking Kaspar Hauser to be, as popular theory supposed, the wronged heir to a noble house occupied himself energetically with trying to establish his origin. He also agreed with the City of Nuremberg to relieve them of their charge and adopted the boy himself, promising him a home in England, but for the time being settling him with a tutor to continue his education.

About this time, maybe as the result of the attention he had received, Kaspar Hauser's character began to change for the worse. Previously he had seemed remarkably good-natured, simple and unassuming. His early teachers had found him obedient and quick to learn. Now, however, he became petulant and vain. He declared he hated women, vicars, doctors and cats (who however were ceaselessly fascinated by him). The theory that he was perhaps of royal blood, the victim of some court intrigue, appealed strongly to him, although there was absolutely no evidence for it. Finally even Lord Stanhope grew tired of him and proposed that he be found a post in some office. It was at this period that the final tragedy took place. Kaspar Hauser received a note at his office requesting that he keep an assignation at the public gardens. He set out, but shortly afterwards staggered home wounded in the chest. He had, he said, been stabbed by the same man, the man who had taken him from his cell the first day he came into the world. On 17 December 1832 he died.

For the whole of the rest of the century interest in the case persisted. One party took Lord Stanhope as the villain, an adventurer in the pay of a corrupt court, even as the murderer. Lord Stanhope himself published some peevish letters to show his belief that Kaspar Hauser was some sort of impostor. His daughter, the Duchess of Cleveland, had the original witnesses to the Foundling's first appearance re-examined to induce them to change their stories. Fantastic speculation that he was the rightful heir to the throne of Baden was followed by law suits and slander trials. The medium, D. D. Home, even summoned up Kaspar Hauser's spirit, who confirmed the Baden theory, one to which he had been greatly attracted during his lifetime. A final odd feature of the story was that nearly everyone connected with Kaspar Hauser died within a short time of the boy himself.

It may be that the real solution to the Kaspar Hauser mystery was hit upon by von Feuerbach, the President of a Bavarian court, who was one of the first to interest himself in the problem. In his book, published in 1834 on Kaspar Hauser he said, ' . . . he exhibited such extraordinary peculiarities in all the characteristics of his mental, moral and physical existence, as seemed to leave us no other choice, than either to regard him as the inhabitant of some other planet, miraculously transferred to the earth, or as one who (like the man whom Plato supposes) had been born and bred under ground, and who, now that he had arrived at the age of maturity, had for the first time ascended to the surface of the earth, and beheld the light of the sun'.

The second of these two alternatives, the one given by Kaspar Hauser himself, and one which he obviously believed to be true, is not, of course practical. It is hardly possible to imagine a cell, such as Kaspar Hauser described, where no noise, not even of thunder, penetrated, yet with two blocked up windows and a supply of fresh air sufficient to keep a boy alive. It is even more difficult to imagine in the remote Bavarian countryside in the early nineteenth century before the days of electricity how a room could be kept at an even temperature and evenly lit with no obvious apparatus for making it so. Even if it were possible, it is hard to see any conceivable reason for acting in this way. There is one place, however, which would fit all the conditions which Kaspar Hauser described – a cell in an object moving through space, an interplanetary vehicle, within which Kaspar Hauser together with one or more other passengers had for many years been travelling through a silent universe.

If a people living outside the earth wanted to put one of their number into human society, the best person to choose would be one who had no knowledge of any previous existence. A baby, like the first Prince of Wales knowing nothing of his own language, who could be kept alive during a long space flight, would never be able to betray his origins. He could be observed and tested from time to time to see how he adapted himself to human conditions. It may have been thought that upon awakening from a monotonous seventeen years in a dimly lit, evenly heated craft moving through the silence of space, the boy would feel as if born into the human race and find his place as an unobtrusive member of it. The few dialect words, which may have been all his controllers knew, would be sufficient education for him to find a position.

It is interesting to compare Kaspar Hauser with the children of Woolpit. Both were young and both appeared mysteriously just outside a town. Neither Kaspar nor the children could speak nor, later, give any clear account of where they had come from. The children were first aware of the sound of church bells; the same sound woke Kaspar Hauser out of the daze in which he first arrived. In both cases the foundlings were not entirely like human beings, but they all adapted themselves in the course of time; the children lost their green colour, Kaspar Hauser's features became human, his extraordinary senses, which could hardly have been developed as the result of a long spell in an underground cell, came into conformity with human standards, and even his saliva, thick and sticky as glue when he first appeared, took on a normal consistency.

Another peculiar thing, the hardest of all to express, was that Kaspar Hauser, like the Orford 'merman' and the Woolpit children were, as Jung said of the post-war flying saucers, in some way expected. At least they came in a form which was not quite outside the experience of people of their times. In the Middle Ages fairy children were known from rumour or legend. Their appearance, though sensational, was explicable. The 'merman' too was not unique. All round the coast of Scotland, there were stories of creatures half-human half-seal, the seal-woman who, when her skin was stolen by a man, had to become his wife until she could get it back, sea monsters and the like. These creatures were phenomenal but not impossible and would not therefore cause panic or demoralisation. The same is true of Kaspar Hauser. People of the nineteenth century were yearning for mysteries. Here was a figure on which they could fasten all their fantasies. Half supernatural, half charlatanesque, the perfect romantic hero for his time, he was ideally conceived to drive people's minds in the direction they already wanted to go. Like flying saucers themselves he was, maybe, a portent, a figure of far greater significance than has yet been allowed.

If Kaspar Hauser was a visitor from space his mission was a failure, almost a disaster. It had probably been assumed that after the first excitement had died down, he would be accepted as an ordinary human being. In fact this never happened. He was taken up by scientists, tested and examined and made the subject of speculation, some of it, like Feuerbach's, of a highly pertinent nature. For him to be recognised as an experimental being from outside the earth would have been calamitous. Feuerbach, who came close to doing so, died suddenly while in his prime shortly after publishing his book. Before his death the first attempt on the life of Kaspar Hauser had been made. After that the boy was closely watched and it was some time before he could finally be destroyed.

In view of what had happened in the past, it was perhaps not unreasonable for whoever directed him to assume that Kaspar Hauser's arrival would cause little stir. Creatures not unlike him had long been known to appear and had been accepted as belonging to the familiar semi-human race of 'wild men'. If Kaspar Hauser was a more evolved example of a wild man, he was by no means the first. These creatures were supposed in the Middle Ages to haunt the woods, deserts and wildernesses. For this reason their appearance usually failed to cause the panic which a less familiar monster would have done. Because their type was known, they were accepted as natural members of a world divided between human beings and supernatural creatures. In this way, they were able at times to enter human society and become accepted as ordinary men. The belief was that a wild man captured could be humanised by the love of a woman. Stories of this happening were not uncommon particularly in Germany and Scandinavia. The disguise of a wild man would therefore be a particularly suitable one for a being of alien origin who wanted to infiltrate a human community without his unhuman characteristics causing any particular surprise or alarm.

Later, as belief in the wild man declined, so did people's tolerance towards him. There is a story that one such creature appeared in a remote Derbyshire village during the Napoleonic wars, and was immediately put to death. In the usual form in which the story is told, as a joke at the expense of country people, the creature was an ape, for some reason wandering about the English countryside. The villagers, it is said, took him for a Frenchman, a Napoleonic spy. As such he was tried, sentenced to death and executed. The point of the story, that nineteenth-century English country people could not tell a monkey from a Frenchman, is not of course to be taken seriously. Far more likely, the villagers killed the semi-human monster because they suspected something of its alien origin. They then covered what they had done in the traditional way by representing themselves as ignorant rustics.

The last of the old type of wild men was probably Peter the 'Wild Boy of Berkhamsted'. He also, like Kaspar Hauser, was found in Germany, near Hamelin, when he was apparently about twelve years old. King George II and Queen Caroline took an interest in the boy who was wild, hairy and incapable of speech. They had him brought to England and lodged him at a farm near Berkhamsted in Hertfordshire where he spent his life roaming far about the countryside. Peter lived to an old age, and when he died a monument was put up to him which can still be seen in a local church.

It is unlikely that Peter was anything more than a poor simpleton who had wandered away from his home in Brunswick and never learnt to talk enough to give an account of himself. But the way he was accepted and the royal interest in his welfare show the degree of tolerance with which such creatures were treated. It may be that Kaspar Hauser appeared as a speechless rustic of this sort in order to spare him the hostility of the people of Nuremberg. If so, his effort was too successful for the success of his mission, in direct contrast to the ape-man in the English village. But, in general, since the 'wild man' was accepted as a natural phenomenon in spite of his supernatural associations, any inhuman or extra-terrestrial creature who needed to assume a conventional character while on earth would have found it convenient to play the part.

If infiltration into the human race does go on, one of the most obvious ways in which it is done is that described by John Wyndham in his novel *The Midwich Cuckoos*. Children, fathered by an extra-terrestrial force appear on earth and threaten by their vastly superior intelligence to conquer the world. The horror of this idea derives of course from its connection with the archetypal belief in the changeling. The fear that a young baby may be stolen away and replaced by a fairy child is deep rooted, so much so that it can not be explained as having been prompted by the occasional appearance of a sickly baby or a mongol. Also, it is not only babies who are changed. In the Irish countryside where such things are noticed, Yeats and Lady Gregory collected many examples of sick or moody people whose real self was said to be 'away'. They were possessed for the time by an alien spirit.

An awareness of changelings is widely found in Celtic countries and there are innumerable ways laid down of foiling them or compelling them to reverse the exchange. One of the best ways was to bewilder or amuse the changeling so that it gave itself away and could no longer impersonate a human child. A Welsh woman in Montgomery had twins who would not grow and gave other signs of having been changed. She was advised to play a trick on them. Just before the men returned from the harvest field, she took half an egg shell, put some stew into it, and set it on the fire saying, 'That will do nicely for the men's dinner'. The changelings were amazed. One turned to the other and said,

'Gwelais fesen cyn gweled derwen
Gwelais wy cyn gweled iar,
Erioed ni welais ferwi bwyd i fedel
Mewn plisgyn wy iar!'

which according to the Rev. Elias Owen, the author of *Welsh Folklore*, means,

'Acorns before oak I knew,
An egg before a hen,
Never one hen's egg-shell stew
Enough for harvest men!'

The changelings then vanished and the real babies appeared in their place. This belief that alien creatures could take over the body of a baby was so persistent that as late as 1884 two women were charged in Ireland with placing a baby on a red hot shovel in the belief that it was a changeling. Many such stories were told to Lady Gregory when she was travelling in the West of Ireland, a land where there has always been a strong awareness of the supernatural race.

'There was an old man on the road one night near Burren and he heard a cry in the air over his head, the cry of a child that was being carried away. And he called out some words and the child was let down into his arms and he brought it home. And when he got there he was told that it was dead. So he brought in the live child, and you may be sure that it was some sort of a thing that was good for nothing that was put in its place.

It's the good and the handsome they take, and those that are of use, or whose name is up for some good action. Idlers they don't like, but who would like Idlers?'

The belief that a man's body may be taken over by an alien spirit is everywhere well known. One curious version is that which forms the legend of the doppelgänger, a figure most frequently found in Germany, but occurring in Ireland and elsewhere. The doppelgänger is the exact double of a living person. It may exist at the same time as the person it is imitating, but the appearance of a man's doppelgänger always brings about his death, whether it appears to him or to another person. In some cases the doppelgänger goes on living after its human model is dead. This has led to apparently inexplicable reports of people being seen after they are dead and cases where two versions of the same man have been met in widely separated places at the same time. One of the most remarkable examples of the substitution of one man for another was the case of the murder of von Veltheim in 1897.

Von Veltheim had recently arrived in England from Australia, where he had left his wife, and had entered into a bigamous marriage with a Greek lady he met in London. The Australian wife, however, pursued him and exposed him to the Greek lady, whereupon von Veltheim, to avoid legal complications, made himself scarce.

Some time later he was found murdered and trussed up with ropes, floating in the Thames. It was impossible to mistake him. Von Veltheim was six foot four inches tall, with enormously broad shoulders and athletic development. His head was noticeably small, but he was good looking with dark brown eyes and hair. He had a gold filling in one tooth and a small, clipped moustache.

In view of his striking appearance the police were confident that the dead man would soon be identified. Yet for some time no one came forward to claim him. Finally the Australian Mrs von Veltheim read a description in the newspaper and after seeing the body positively identified it as that of her husband. The murderers, she said, must be the relations of the second wife, who had come over from Greece to help her in her trouble. It was partly through fear of them that von Veltheim had gone into hiding.

This, however, was as far as inquiries could be taken, for von Veltheim himself or a creature calling himself by that name and with exactly the same striking appearance, turned up in South Africa. He said he knew nothing about the murdered man, his exact double, and no further clue to the identity of the corpse ever emerged. But the doppelgänger in South Africa embarked on a sinister career. As von Veltheim he was charged with the murder of Woolf Joel, one of the owners of the Kimberley diamond mines in partnership with Solly Joel and Barney Barnato. The death of Barnato, who fell, jumped or was pushed off a liner in mid-Atlantic, and the murder of Woolf Joel left Solly Joel as sole owner. For some reason von Veltheim was found not guilty of the murder, but he was later sentenced to twenty years penal servitude for demanding money with menaces from Solly Joel in England. After serving five years he was released and deported and nothing more was heard of him.

One thing in this story seems quite clear. The murdered man found in the Thames was the original version of von Veltheim. His appearance was quite distinctive. It is impossible to imagine that two such men could have existed in London at the same time, that one of them should have been so entirely unknown that his much publicised description should have produced nobody to identify him. Until the second version turned up in Africa it occurred to nobody that the corpse could be that of anyone but von Veltheim. His wife identified him, and so did the landlord of a house where von Veltheim had stayed. Moreover there was a good reason to expect his murder. The Greek relations of the second wife had come to England on purpose to avenge her, and there is little doubt that they were, in fact, responsible for the murder. The mystery is who the person could have been who later impersonated von Veltheim, where he came from, and the purpose of the murder which, under the name of von Veltheim, was committed in Africa.

In view of the many varied cases, some mentioned above, of aliens appearing on earth and of human beings 'possessed' by alien spirits, it may be that Dr Cleary Baker's view of the imminence of an extra-terrestrial coup is over-simple. This sort of thing has been going on for a long time, and we have always been partly conscious of it. Yet if there is extra-terrestrial life, it is unlikely to be long before, with our scientific advance, we come into contact with it. Moreover our culture is reaching a climax, expanding inside terrestrial limits which will soon no longer be able to contain it. When our present moral and social institutions collapse, an entirely new inspiration will be needed to help us to create new ones. This inspiration can only come, as it has at the start of new ages in the past, from outside. We may expect alien ideas, perhaps alien visitors. What our attitude to them will be it is now impossible to say. Debate on whether they will be 'hostile' or 'friendly' is irrelevant and meaningless; people who talk of an invasion or 'take-over' are thinking in purely terrestrial terms. Our contact with extra-terrestrial life is likely to come so gradually that by the time we have openly to face it, we will be entirely conditioned to accept it.

We are now on the verge of a period of great change, such as has occurred in the past. If we can understand something of the events which led up to the first coming of the gods and the impact of these events on primitive men, we may be better able to evaluate certain strange incidents which are occurring today.

CHAPTER FIVE

The Lover from the Sky

In the Autumn of 1966 *Look* magazine and the *Sunday Mirror* printed extracts from a book by John G. Fuller, *The Interrupted Journey,* which describes the adventure of a young American couple with a flying saucer. Driving across country by night something had happened to them which they were subsequently unable to recall, but which for some time afterwards had caused them uneasiness and physical pain. In the case of the man, Barney Hill, the pain occurred in the lower abdomen and groin. Finally, the couple consulted a doctor who sent them to a psychiatrist, and in the course of treatment they were both able to remember the details of their experience.

According to their story they had, in the course of their drive, become aware of a bright, glowing object in the sky following their car. The object came to the ground and the Hills saw it was some sort of aircraft or, as they said, flying saucer, blazing with light and with a double row of portholes round its circumference. Some men emerged from the saucer, drew the Hills from their car and led them inside. The couple were then separated and each subjected to a detailed medical examination involving, in the case of Mr Hill, at least, some sort of sex test. They were then allowed to leave the saucer and return to the car, but the memory of what had happened was blotted out from their minds and only brought back by hypnotic treatment at the psychiatrist's.

This story, sensational enough in itself, becomes even more significant when compared with other reports of the same sort of thing occurring on occasions within the last few years. Of all the thousands of flying saucer reports and claims of contact with their occupants, a few stick in the mind either because of some vividness in their detail or because they seem to fit into the general pattern of behaviour with which flying saucers are becoming associated. The most startling of the many legends, which have gathered round the

77

creatures from flying saucers, is that one of their reasons for coming to earth is to create a hybrid race, people with the intelligence and knowledge of the extra-terrestrial, but physically adapted to life on earth. Those who believe that this may now be taking place, that men may on occasions be used in genetic experiments by extra-terrestrials, were confirmed in their behalf by an incident which occurred in Brazil in 1957. This incident, which was first reported in 1962 by Dr W. Buhler in a Brazilian magazine, came to the attention of Mr Gordon Creighton who published details of it in 1965 in the *Flying Saucer Review*. The *Review* has since received further details of this fascinating story from those who first investigated it and its later issues provide a full report of what is here given only in outline.

On 14 December 1957 very late in the evening two brothers were ploughing a field on their farm in a remote part of the country when they noticed a light in the sky apparently following their movements. When it began to approach nearer they were scared and made for home. The next night one of the brothers went to work in the field alone. The same light appeared, this time hovering directly overhead. The farmer tried to uncouple the tractor from the plough in order to drive away, but the hydraulic gear failed to work. The next moment the engine of the tractor cut out and would not restart. The light in the sky suddenly swooped down to the ground and the farmer saw a circular object standing on three legs alongside his tractor. A number of small men climbed out of the object, seized the farmer and dragged him inside. They carefully removed his clothes, took, apparently, a sample of blood from his chin and moistened his body with a sponge. He was then led into another compartment inside the craft and laid down on a sort of plastic bed. The men withdrew, leaving the farmer lying on the bed alone. Some minutes later he became aware of a disgusting smell, and was violently sick. A door in the compartment opened, and two of the men came in leading a naked woman under five foot in height. The farmer later described her as being in some way Chinese or Slavonic looking. She had thin blonde hair, but no eyebrows or eyelashes and no other hair on her body.

She went up to the farmer on the bed, seduced him without speaking and then left the compartment. The farmer went out into the room where he had left his clothes, dressed, and was taken by one of the men out on to a platform which ran all the way round the craft and down a ladder to the ground. He was able to look at the craft, which was like a great dome on stilts before it suddenly took off at great speed. The place where it had stood could clearly be seen by the marks on the ground.

When asked what he thought of his experience the farmer said he was very frightened. Moreover he had since married and did not like to talk too much about what had happened. For some weeks afterwards he suffered from ulcers on his face and arms and from a feeling of sickness. It was later found that he was suffering from exposure to radiation, presumably from his contact with an extra-terrestrial object. However he admitted, 'If it should happen again that the same machine with the same people landed once more, I would not run away'.

Those who first investigated the farmer's story decided not to reveal publicly all the details, particularly those relating to the construction of the craft, in order to compare them with any further reports of the same type. It now appears that similar incidents have since occurred, for there have been other reports from South America and one very odd case in France.

The story of what happened at Valensole on 1 July 1965 has never been satisfactorily explained. The farmer, M. Masse, certainly had a terrifying experience and suffered effects similar to those described by Mr and Mrs Hill in America and by the Brazilian. Very early one morning M. Masse, while working in the lavender fields, saw a strange object descend from the sky. A French newspaper quoted the story he gave to the police.

'At a distance of about thirty metres from me, I saw a strange machine the shape of which vaguely recalled a rugby ball. Its size was approximately that of a Dauphine car, and it was of a dull colour. It was standing on four sort of metallic legs and a central support. It looked like a monstrous great spider. On the ground, there was a human being of the height and build of a child of about eight. He was wearing a one-piece suit, but no helmet, and his hands were bare. Inside the machine I could see another being.'

M. Masse and his family have been strangely reluctant to say what happened next before the machine and its occupants finally disappeared, but Charles Bowen, the editor of *Flying Saucer Review*, commenting on the original report by Aimé Michel, suggested that M. Masse underwent some kind of sexual experience which he is not anxious to reveal and perhaps, like the Hills, cannot exactly recall. But experiences of this sort have not, it seems, been confined to the present day. In many parts of the world there are stories from the past, legends of a union between a man from earth and a woman from outside. It is by comparison with these legends that the modern reports of erotic encounters with people from space become so significant.

The North American Indians have several such stories. An Algonkin legend tells of a hunter who, wandering through a forest, came across a clearing covered with rich grass. In the middle of the clearing was a great circle where the grass had been crushed down. What puzzled the hunter was that there was no track leading up to the circle, and he was unable to understand what had caused it. He therefore hid in the undergrowth to see what might happen. Some time later a circular object appeared overhead and then landed, exactly fitting the outline on the grass. Twelve beautiful girls climbed out of the vehicle and began to dance in the clearing. The hunter rushed out of his hiding place, but as soon as they saw him they re-entered their craft and, by singing a certain chant, took off into the sky.

The man was so struck by the lovely girls that he spent much of his time by the circle, hoping that they would return. When at last they did so, the hunter was able by a trick to capture one of them. He held on to her as her sisters flew off in their craft, took her home and lived with her for some years, during which time she had a son.

One day the wife had a longing to see her home again. While the hunter was out she made a circular basket like the vehicle in which she and her sisters had arrived, sat in it with her baby, and sung the chant which caused them to ascend into the air.

The hunter was miserable when he returned home and found the woman and child gone. For a long time he haunted the clearing in the forest, hoping she would come back. Meanwhile the boy who had gone with his mother to her home in the sky was beginning to want his father. Seeing this, the ruler of the country, the woman's father, told her to go down to earth and bring the hunter back with her. But before he came, he was to kill a specimen of every creature which he normally hunted, and take a part of each specimen up into the sky with him.

The woman went down to earth, landing in the circle, found the

80

DRAGON HILLS

I Many of the beacons and hills across the country were said to be haunted by a fiery flying dragon. On Herefordshire Beacon can be seen earthworks of the sort sometimes said to be marks made by the dragon's coils.

II The Berkshire White Horse, perfectly visible only from the air, points with its neck towards the sacred enclosure, Uffington Castle, and with its tail to Dragon Hill, where, on the ever grassless summit, St George killed the dragon.

III The form of a giant serpent, discernible only from the sky, appears in Britain at such places as Avebury and Callernish; also in the serpentine mounds of Scotland and North America. In this example from Ohio the disc, like the serpent a symbol of the airship of the gods, appears in the serpent's jaws.

V The traditional forms of Tibetan Buddhist architecture express the relationship of the gods and their vehicle. The figure inside the perforated dome or wheel is a fundamental feature of all eastern religions and occurs in Christian iconography.

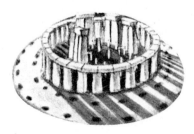

VI Stonehenge, seen from above as in this reconstruction from the Ministry of Works guide book, represents the traditional form of the gods' sky disc and unmistakably resembles photographs and drawings of recent UFOs. The smaller blue stones within the stone circle may have been standing elsewhere at the time the main structure was built and imported as representing the figures of the gods.

IV The gods inside the spinning disc. Divination Wheel' in the British Museum.

VII Illustration from the Winchester Bible of the vision in Ezekiel X of flying wheels and men from the sky.

VIII It has often been rumoured that an alien spacecraft has crashed on earth or been captured by the authorities. Possible evidence for a UFO disaster can be seen in the vast destructive explosion over Siberia in 1908. More startling is the frequently repeated story that President Eisenhower during a supposed golfing trip actually inspected a captured UFO. This photograph, said to be of one of the dead crew of a flying saucer which crashed in Germany, was published in the 1950's.

IX Anne Bodenham's spirits. This 17th century vision of alien creatures shows them with horns or antennae, a feature common to prehistoric carved figures such as those from Sardinia and extra-terrestrials in modern comics. As usual the vehicle is the fiery disc.

X In the early 19th century the explorer Grey copied this figure from a rock in the Glenelg River country of Western Australia. What appears to be an inscription on a halo or helmet has never been deciphered, but the characters are curiously similar to certain marks found on rocks in South America and also very like the letters of the message which George Adamski claimed to have received from his Venusian visitor. Similar figures appear on the walls of early Ethiopian churches.

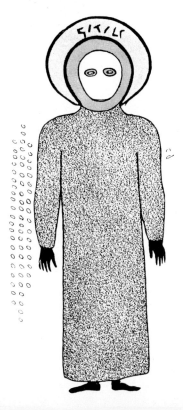

XI A group of 'Wondjina', ancestor gods of the Aborigines of the Kimberley district. These figures, restored each year by the Aborigines but, they say, originally painted by the gods themselves, represent an advanced people with whom the Aborigines once had contact and who now ride in the strange lights which they see in the sky by night.

XIII The post-war discovery by a French expedition of the remarkably
preserved prehistoric painting in the Sahara desert encouraged those who
believe in surviving portraits of spacemen in the past. This giant god was
called 'The Martian' by expedition members.

II A painted rock surface in the Sahara shows a number of flying men
nd objects including this figure.

WEST · EAST

ENGLAND FROM THE AIR

XIV Miss Maltwood's rediscovery of the zodiacal giants of Somerset on the plain beneath Glastonbury Tor has been a notable step in the modern revival of astrology.

XV A photograph by Alfred Watkins, discoverer of the 'ley' system, showing field gates aligned on a hilltop, the only trace now visible of one of the mysterious straight tracks of the prehistoric landscape.

hunter and returned to the sky with him and his specimens. A feast was prepared where all the guests received something of what the hunter had brought. After the feast they all became transformed and each took the form of the animal or bird he had eaten. The hunter, his wife and child became a giant falcon and flew off into the sky.

It is evident that all these stories and legends have certain features in common. For one thing, they all have as their climax the appearance of a flying saucer. In the Indian legend the vessel is described in the simplest terms as a round basket, while in the modern examples it stands on legs. But in three cases, including the Indian version, it left a mark on the ground where it had stood. This was particularly emphasised at Valensole, where the imprint of the object that frightened the farmer was compared at the time to the mark left by the thing from the sky which landed in Wiltshire in 1963. A recent report from Queensland also associated mysteriously circular depressions in the ground with the activities of flying saucers.

But the main interest of these stories is not so much in the flying objects as in their inhabitants, particularly in the purpose for which they came to earth. In two cases at least, those of the Brazilian farmer and the Indian hunter, the woman who appeared from the sky formed a union with a man on earth. In the case of the Brazilian, as with Mr Hill, the object of their captors was to conduct some sort of sexual experiment. The farmer was seduced under clinical conditions and Mr Hill had some kind of instrument applied to his groin in a way that seems to indicate that a specimen of his semen was taken. Like the girl in the story of the Indian hunter, who took her baby back with her into the sky, the woman in the Brazilian flying saucer may have intended to conceive a hybrid creature, one of a race capable of colonising the earth.

Accounts of sexual union in the past between men and extra-terrestrials are by no means rare. In one form, like that of the Indian hunter, they occur all over the world. Sometimes the image of the flying saucer has disappeared, and the women appear as birds, the swan-maidens of Aryan mythology, or as animals, particularly seals. Here a man captures one of the women as his bride by stealing her swan feather cloak or sealskin while she is bathing. She then has to stay with him until she can escape by finding the skin which the man had taken from her. When she leaves earth, she takes her half-human child with her.

In later folklore the flying saucer or any means of leaving the face of the earth is not mentioned and the woman, the 'fairy bride', vanishes in a supernatural manner as the result of her man breaking some taboo or condition she has laid upon him. He must not, for example, strike her without cause, reproach her or touch her with iron. When finally he does one of these things the woman vanishes. Wild Edric, an English patriot in rebellion against William the Conqueror, was the hero of one such story. While wandering in the Forest of Dean he came upon an inn. Inside was a party of beautiful girls dancing. They were obviously not of the human race. Wild Edric caught hold of one of them and dragged her outside despite the resistance of her sisters. She agreed to be his wife on condition that he never reproached her with her family or origin. For some time all went well. Edric became reconciled to King William and presented his unearthly bride at court, where she was very popular. But one day after he had looked for her and had been unable to find her for some time, he said to her, 'I suppose you have been spending your time with your sisters', whereupon she vanished for ever.

The legends of erotic encounters with extra-terrestrials and the modern accounts of seductive creatures from flying saucers show the strength of the tradition that sexual contact can take place between men and members of an alien race. In some modern versions the experience is said to be rather frightening; yet in the past, life with a fairy bride was considered to be one of unimaginable pleasure. Sometimes, as with Tannhäuser in the Venusberg, the state of continual ecstasy was unendurable. But in all the religions which succeeded the departure of the gods, a strong element in the great yearning for new contact with the divine beings was the desire for the alien bride, the holy virgin, the attendant of the Grail.

Among some people the first contact with the gods and their superior technology was said to have been made through an alliance between members of the two races. A Maori legend describes how the gods first became known to men through a man of the alien race who married the daughter of a Maori chief. The girl, Hine-rangi, was destined for a life of religious chastity, and she was isolated from the rest of her people in a hut outside the village. It caused surprise, therefore, when she was seen to be pregnant. When questioned about her lover, the girl declared that he was no ordinary man, but came down from the sky. He only visited her after dark and left before morning. This made it difficult for the chief and his people to catch him, but finally they thought of a plan. They went round Hine-rangi's hut and blocked up any hole through which the least chink of light could enter, so that when her lover awoke in the morning, he would not know that dawn was breaking. The trick worked. The visitor was still in Hiner-angi's hut at midday, when the people burst in and captured him. He said his name was Miru, and he was the son of the chief of the country in the sky. He was quite willing to marry Hine-rangi. Impressed by his appearance the Maori chief consented to the marriage, and the couple lived happily for some time, Hine-rangi producing a son.

At last Miru decided he wanted to visit his old home, and he invited the chief, his father-in-law and a small party to accompany him, including his own son and the younger daughter, Hine-rangi's sister. When they arrived at Miru's home, the Maoris were amazed at what they saw, a civilisation far ahead of theirs, great stone houses, and a people skilled in astronomy and other branches of science. Miru offered to teach the Maori party something of the arts which his people knew. The chief was so pleased that when his visit was over he left his younger daughter to be Miru's wife.

Hine-rangi was inconsolable when she heard that her sister had taken her place with her husband. But she was the only one who failed to benefit from her father's visit to the sky-country, for the chief and his grandson taught the people all that they had learnt of the civilisation they had just visited. Maori tradition is that upon this their present culture was founded.

Ethnologists believe that this story contains a true memory of a superior race with whom the Maoris were once in contact and who did in fact introduce them to a high plane of civilisation, from which they subsequently lapsed. It belongs to that part of universal mythology which describes the first contact between men and gods, the institution of human civilisation which the meeting produced, and the creation of a hybrid race, a bridge between gods and men.

This theme, the unions between gods and men, is, of course, basic in all mythology. One version occurs in those verses from Genesis VI often quoted as evidence of past visits to earth by an extra-terrestrial race,

'And it came to pass, when men began to multiply on the face of the earth, and daughters were born unto them,

That the sons of God saw the daughters of men that they were fair; and they took them wives of all which they chose.

And the Lord said, My spirit shall not always strive with man, for that he also is flesh: yet his days shall be an hundred and twenty years.

There were giants on the earth in those days; and also after that, when the sons of God came in unto the daughters of men, and they bare children unto them, the same became mighty men which were of old, men of renown.'

A well-known story from Greek mythology concerned with sexual union between men and gods is that of Ixion, a favourite of Zeus. His downfall came about when he tried to make love to the wife of Zeus, Hera, and was tricked into thinking that he had done so by Zeus who substituted a cloud for his wife. From the union of Ixion and the cloud was produced an unnatural monster, the first of the centaurs. Ixion was punished by being tied to a circular object, later depicted as a sort of wheel, and sent spinning through the heavens.

The most interesting of all the types of erotic space visitors is the beautiful woman descending to earth in a disc-shaped vehicle. The memory of this divine bride is so deep-rooted, that it would be surprising if there were no modern reports of her appearance. In fact there is a considerable number. The most striking is the event which took place at Fatima in 1917. The thousands who saw the lady and the shining, spinning disc descend from the sky put the facts of what happened beyond dispute, though the Christian interpretation which the miracle naturally attracted, may hide the lady's true purpose and the meaning of her appearance.

The visions appeared first of all to three children, Lucia aged ten and her cousin Francisco and Jacita who were nine and seven. They lived in a bleak and remote area of Portugal and their parents were poor peasants who brought their children up strong in the Catholic faith. From the time they were quite young the three children spent much of their day wandering about the barren countryside near their homes. Here they began to have ecstatic religious experiences which they saw as a preparation for some great task they would have to fulfil. Several times a young man, incredibly beautiful, translucent, streaming with light appeared to them. On 13 May 1917 they had the first of their great visions. Above a small tree in a lonely valley they saw a globe of light. Inside the globe stood a lady. To the children she was the incarnation of the Virgin Mary, dressed in white and more brilliant to look at than the sun. She spoke to the children and said she came from heaven. She left with them a message of consolation and then began to glide away in her luminous globe. The children watched until she was out of sight.

Exactly a month later the lady appeared again. This time a small group of people from neighbouring villages went with the children to witness the vision. They heard the lady as she spoke to the eldest child, Lucia, but could not make out her words which sounded 'like the buzzing of a bee'.

As news of their visions began to be known, the children came in for a great deal of particularly vicious persecution. Their own families called them blasphemous liars and the local priest told them they had been guilty of communicating with devils. For most of the six months that the visions lasted the attitude of the Church towards the children and their story was one of suspicion and wariness with occasional bouts of bullying. A wave of anti-clericalism was sweeping Portugal and it was thought imprudent to claim as a holy miracle the visions of children who, if they were discredited, would bring the Church further into disrepute. But the hostility of the priests – the few sympathisers were among the Jesuits – was equalled by that of the civil authorities. On her third appearance the lady had taken Lucia aside and told her a secret which she had promised never to reveal. The civil administrator of the district, a bloodthirsty revolutionary who had seized power locally, went so far as to kidnap the children, lock them in a cell and threaten them with death unless they told him the secret. He took the two youngest one by one out of the cell and told Lucia that he had boiled them in oil and would treat her the same if she continued to hold out. But finally, defeated, he had to release the children. During their imprisonment the time for the lady's fourth visit had passed. However she appeared to them shortly afterwards and told them that something remarkable would happen on her last appearance on 13 October.

By the time the day came of the lady's fifth appointment with the children, the news of what was happening had spread far and wide and a great crowd were waiting to see the vision. Among the crowd was a party of thirty students from an ecclesiastical college and five or

85

six priests. One of them, Monsignor Joao Quaresma wrote a description of what he saw.

'At midday a complete silence, save for the whispering of prayers, fell over the crowd. Suddenly there were shouts of rejoicing. . . . Arms went up to point to something above. . . . To my astonishment I saw clearly and distinctly a luminous globe that moved from the east towards the west, slowly and majestically gliding down across the distance. My friend also looked and had the good fortune to enjoy the same unexpected and enchanting apparition. . . . Suddenly the globe with its extraordinary light vanished before our eyes.'

The news of this apparition, seen by so many people, soon became known all over Portugal, and on 13 October exactly, a month later, some 70,000 people came together at Fatima to see the miracle promised for that date. At midday occurred one of the most amazing events of all times. The day was wet and overcast. Suddenly through the clouds there appeared a great, shining, silver disc, brighter than the sun but easily gazed at by the naked eye. As the crowd watched, it began to 'dance' moving across the sky 'like a globe of snow revolving on itself'. As it spun a bright red glow appeared on its rim. The sky was lit up and the faces of the people looking upwards shone with its brilliance. Other colours followed, green, red, orange, blue and violet; then, spinning rapidly, the disc began to approach the earth until those below felt the warmth of its glow. For some minutes it hung in the air just above the crowd and then it shot upwards, moving in a zig-zag fashion towards the overcast sky.

One of the puzzling features of the events at Fatima was that, while the luminous globe or disc in the sky was seen on more than one occasion, and on its last appearance by a crowd of 70,000, no one except the children is reliably said to have seen the lady. Of the disc there can be no doubt. It was one of those apparitions, perhaps the easiest of all to 'prove' within our present conventions, which have been seen so often both before and since. The spinning, silver disc, the warmth in the air, the enigmatic behaviour of the object itself are all familiar from flying saucer reports. But it was not the vehicle which most attracted the attention of the children; it was the lady associated with it, whom they named the Virgin Mary. Although none but the children saw her, she was evidently as much present as was the disc or globe. She spoke, arranged appointments and gave the children a secret message which they showed themselves unwilling to reveal even with death as the alternative. There is a sort of fairy tale atmosphere about the whole story. The lady appears to have been one of those supernatural figures like the attendant of the Holy Grail who can appear to one person and be invisible to another. She revealed herself above or by a tree like the angels who visited Joan of Arc or like the legendary local goddesses of pre-Christian Portugal. This was one of the reasons why the Church was always suspicious of the miracle and of the lady herself. In some ways she seemed to have less in common with the modern concept of the Virgin Mary than with certain older figures, whose memory the priests had still not entirely suppressed. It is possible to see in her one more example of the revival of pre-Christian forms, a phenomenon now closely associated, as was the Fatima lady herself, with the appearance of flying saucers. Now that Christianity has lost its monopoly in interpreting supernatural events, a great many older beliefs, long suppressed, are beginning to re-emerge. Figures once universally known, but for long ignored or presented in purely Christian terms, are reappearing in their old form and with something of their old meaning. The works of the post-war American flying saucer visionaries are full of references to the erotic space woman, displayed in her pristine character and no longer as the conventional figure of angel or succubus. Since most of these works borrow deeply from the fantasy of their authors, their value is not strictly historical. But they are interesting as an indication of renewed obsessions with beliefs long dormant, whose revival may help us to understand the great changes we must soon expect, and to adapt our way of thinking to meet them.

The underlying erotic character of the space visitors of the 1950s is a feature of all the works in which they appear. The literary tradition which their coming inspired lasted only a short time, from the publication in 1953 of George Adamski's first immensely successful book written in partnership with Desmond Leslie, *Flying Saucers Have Landed* to the death of Adamski himself in 1963. During that time a great deal was written on the subject of the beautiful people from space. The first interplanetary encounter was dramatically described by Adamski.

'It was about 12.30 in the noon hour on Thursday, 20 November 1952, that I first made personal contact with a man from another world. He came to Earth in his space craft, a flying saucer. He called it a Scout Ship.'

The meeting took place in the Californian desert. Adamski whose long career as a mystic and great success in photographing flying saucers had perhaps made him not unprepared for something of the sort to happen, had driven into the desert with a small group of his friends including Dr George Hunt Williamson, who later became a prolific writer on the flying saucer problem. They all shared Adamski's experience; indeed one of the illustrations to *Flying Saucers Have Landed* shows 'Photostatic copies of the original affidavits of the witnesses sworn by them before notaries public'.

After they had driven some distance into the desert, a flying saucer appeared overhead, and then landed. One of the occupants introduced himself as native of Venus. He was wearing ski pants and ox-blood coloured shoes, and his beautiful, wavy, sandy-coloured hair hung to his shoulders. Adamski said of him,

'The beauty of his form surpassed anything I had ever seen. And the pleasantness of his face freed me of all thought of my personal self.

I felt like a little child in the presence of one with great wisdom and much love, and I became very humble within myself.'

Adamski and the space man entered into conversation by the use of signs and by telepathy. As the result of this Adamski learnt that the strangers were friendly and had come to earth because of worries about increased radiation and its effects on the rest of the universe. They were frightened to land in populous areas because the terror they would cause would result in their being torn to pieces by panic-stricken mobs. Questioned about religion, the space man said he believed in God and in the transmigration of souls. He showed Adamski his space craft which was shaped like a glass bell and made of a beautiful translucent material. When Adamski, in spite of a warning, brushed against it, he received a sort of electric shock which numbed his arm. After a further short conversation on philosophical matters, the space man withdrew into his saucer and whirled off into the sky.

Where he had stood Adamski found footmarks containing curious signs and symbols. The interpretation of these, together with an analysis of the benevolent message of the space man exercised the ingenuity of Adamski and his disciples for years to come. The sect which was created out of Adamski's experience was lucky in its leader, who appeared to be highly favoured with the friendship and confidences of the space people. In later books he described space flights on which he had been invited. These included a visit to the moon, which turned out to be perversely hiding her more favourable side from the view of man, for behind the face visible from earth was a bustling populous country with physical features quite unlike those of the lunar landscape we know.

Adamski's later adventures both in space and on earth were lurid and spectacular, and included an episode where for a short time he played a curious part at the court of the Queen of the Netherlands.

Naturally he has often been accused of out-and-out trickery, of making up a story for money; and indeed much of what he wrote was simply absurd. His rather flashy manner and apparent inability to answer a straight question also told against him.

All the same he impressed a number of people in a strange way, including many who considered themselves quite unsusceptible to ideas of the sort he dealt in. There are also some oddly convincing passages in some of his writing. In describing a journey through outer space, he particularly noted the vast number of 'fire-flies', little points of light which danced around his craft. This was written some time before the first Russian astronaut. But when the American, Glenn, returned from his orbit of the earth, he described the 'fire-flies' almost exactly as Adamski had done.

It could be, of course, that Adamski's inclusion of the 'fire-fly' detail was just a great stroke of luck. Yet, from what people who knew him have said about him, it seems probable that Adamski did have some sort of genuine experience which he found bewildering and uncommunicable, but which, together with the mysticism to which he was prone, led him to produce his story. As has undoubtedly happened to other people, the attention which his story attracted drove him to further mental fantasies until he reached the position where he so believed in his whole story that his sincerity impressed others, but was never able to answer without hesitation many of the searching questions put to him. In this way Adamski was like Home, the medium, who, although demonstrably possessing genuine occult powers, which he himself never understood, was still unable to resist amplifying them with conjuring tricks to impress his rich, grand admirers.

The success of Adamski's books inspired other writers, some of whom he sponsored himself, to receive visits from space people. A feature of all these visitors was their erotic nature which, as a concession to popular puritanism, was always expressed as a sort of coy, sexy flirtatiousness. The technique was brought to perfection by a New Jersey sign-writer, Howard Menger.

Menger's *From Outer Space to You* is a really remarkable work, and the temptation to quote at length from it is too great to be resisted; the justification being that Menger's fantasies, purely and unselfconsciously expressed, may shed some light on certain aspects of the flying saucer problem by a comparison of what is imagined, dreamt or made up with what is actually seen or reliably recorded. Particularly interesting is the reversal of the early Christian practice of adapting mythology and popular beliefs to a Christian meaning. In Menger's story Christian elements seem to be included but they are used in the service of a new, or rather revived, belief, the belief that the gods are not just nebulous, omniscient spirits, but members of a race like ours, only infinitely more advanced, who must shortly be expected to make a physical appearance upon earth to lead us up to a higher level of civilisation.

The cover of *From Outer Space to You* shows a beautiful blonde sitting on a rock; she is scantily robed in white, and her hands are outstretched in the attitude of one expounding some enormous wisdom. At her feet sits a little boy. The boy is Howard Menger, and the incident thus illustrated occurred when he was ten.

There was one spot near Howard's home which he always found beautiful and holy. Here one day he met the space-lady. As he describes it,

'There, sitting on a rock by the brook, was the most exquisite woman my young eyes had ever beheld!

The warm sunlight caught the highlights of her long golden hair as it cascaded around her face and shoulders. The curves of her lovely body were delicately contoured – revealed through the translucent material of clothing which reminded me of the habit of skiers.'

90

She turned to him and Howard felt 'a tremendous surge of warmth, love and physical attraction which emanated from her to me'. He listened entranced as she told him things he only half understood, of wars and troubles and of the fate of the human race. She told him how extra-terrestrials like herself were contacting certain people all over the world, that he was one of the chosen, and that he must be prepared to suffer for the cause. Finally she dismissed him and Howard, as he walked away in tears asked,

' "May I look back?"
"Oh yes, Howard, you may look back."
And I did after walking slowly away . . . I ran, sobbing . . . till my wails of a happy kind of sadness grew and filled the forest.'

At all times in his life Howard Menger had seen flying saucers in the sky, but his next contact with a space visitor did not take place until he was grown up. It turned out to be rather embarrassing. Howard had joined the army, and one night two of his buddies asked him to join them in an outing to the local town, Juarez. The way the two others wanted to spend the evening did not appeal to Howard, so he wandered off alone.

'As I walked down the street towards a curio shop I had spotted, a taxi pulled over to the kerb and the driver addressed me in Spanish.
I replied in perhaps the worst Spanish on earth that I did not speak the language and his look showed me he hastily agreed. Then he said something else and pointed to a man in the back seat.
I am afraid the novelty of the occasion quite nonplussed me. Much to my later chagrin I remember the first thing that struck my mind were some of the stories related in the bull sessions back at camp.
The man had long blonde hair which hung over his shoulders. His skin appeared suntanned. The first quick observation showed that he was taller and heavier than the average Mexican.
He spoke to me in English quite pleasantly, though I remember he had a slight Mexican accent.
"I have something to tell you. Would you get into the cab?" he asked, but I demurred, making the excuse I had to find my buddies

and go back to camp; and at the same time I walked on. As I turned he turned and merely said "All right," again quite pleasantly.

When I told the others about it, there were many guffaws; and for several days I was the butt of much good-natured ribbing.'

Not long afterwards Howard met another spaceman disguised in army uniform. They had a good laugh together over the farcical mix-up in Juarez, and the spaceman told Howard his unit would soon leave for Hawaii. This prophecy was duly fulfilled, and it was in Hawaii that Howard had his second meeting with a spacegirl. Following an uncontrollable impulse he had borrowed a jeep and driven out to a wild rocky district where he felt sure he would meet space-people. There stood a beautiful brunette.

'She was dressed in a sort of flowing outfit of pastel shades. Under a kind of flowing tunic, translucent and pinkish, she wore loosely fitted pyjama-type pantaloons. Her tunic floated gracefully around the shapely contours of her body. The warm moist air of the tropical evening seemed to caress her finely moulded features.'

An embarrassing thing then happened. Howard began to feel the 'strong physical attraction one finds impossible to allay when in the presence of these women'.

Fortunately the girl understood what was going on.

' "Oh, Howard," she almost chided, "it's only a natural thing, I feel it myself. It flows from you to me as from me to you." '

However the influence of the natural stream of attraction was resisted by the couple and they enjoyed a conversation of mutual admiration which ended with the girl telling Howard that his unit would soon go to Okinawa, where it might be necessary for him to kill a man in battle.

The omniscience of the space-people, at least so far as military secrets are concerned, was confirmed when these prophecies too were fulfilled. Howard killed some Japanese in the Pacific war, and shortly afterwards was demobilised, returned to his wife and set up business as a sign-writer. For some time he lived happily and prospered, but one day the old restlessness returned and he drove off in the truck to the spot where he had seen the first space-girl so many years ago.

As he stood at the scene of his first vision, a great flash and a wave of heat from the sky made him look up. A ball of fire was racing across the sky.

'It looked like a huge, spinning sun, shining, pulsating and changing colours. It hovered over the field, as I stood watching it, seemingly transfixed.'

As this object approached the earth, it was seen to be a bell-shaped flying saucer. Out of it stepped two men in grey ski-suits with long blonde hair. They were followed by a girl dressed in the customary translucent, pastel-colour, glowing robes. It was the girl who had appeared to Howard Menger at the same spot when he was ten. In the fourteen years since they last met she had not changed in any way at all.

' "Are you actually the girl—the girl on the rock?" I asked.
"Yes I am. The same girl, Howard."
"But you're no older – "
"Oh but I am. Guess Howard, how old I really am."
I just stood there looking at her.
"I'm more than 500 years old. Now you can refute anyone who says a woman tells little falsehoods about her age!"
"But you haven't changed – "
"Of course not."
Then she looked at me, at my entire body, and my face burned. It was something like a visiting relative looking over a small boy to see how much he had grown.
I knew she was gently teasing me as she winked and added, "Oh, but YOU have changed!" '

Prone to shyness as he was, Howard was deeply embarrassed when, in the course of further conversation, the girl told him that since their last meeting he had been under constant observation.

'I turned red again and hung my head.
She laughed.

93

"No you haven't always been a good boy. There have been times when . . ." and she made as if she were going to take a whack at me where people usually sit down. I flinched and recovered my composure. Then I laughed with her.'

When all this business was over the girl delivered her message. Howard had been chosen to spread the word of the space people on earth. His task, he was warned, would be hard and he would meet persecution and derision. Howard swore he was ready to face all that the world could bring against him, whereupon the girl leaned forward and kissed him gently on the cheek.

From then on Howard Menger's life became one of exciting activity. He was continually in touch with space people. They would appear at all times and in all sorts of disguise, sometimes at an arranged meeting place, a spot beside a tree called 'Field Location 2', and sometimes unexpectedly. Among other adventures, Howard had an encounter with a mystical round table, which acted as a sort of interplanetary television set, played beautiful music on a space-piano, although he had never played a note before in his life, and made a tour of ladies' underwear shops to fit out some of his lady space visitors. Unfortunately however, hardly anyone believed him; he even had to suffer the derision of his own family, for his father, even when confronted with some blurred and distorted photographs of space men continued to believe that his son was the victim of delusions. But all this was compensated for by the warmth and love he received from his space friends, and still more by something that happened to him during a public lecture he was attending on flying saucers. There was a girl there whom he recognised as his wife from another life in the past, and she was a native of Venus, the sister of the original girl on the rock, 'tall, lithe, with long blonde wavy hair cascading around her shoulders'. As soon as he had convinced her of her true identity, Howard, who had by now divorced his first wife, married her, and together they have devoted their lives to spreading the philosophy of the saucers.

Howard Menger's book though one of the most entertaining was only one of many such to appear during the 1950s. A truck driver Truman Bethurum, described his experiences with the captain of a space ship he met in the Nevada desert. Like Howard Menger's girls she was pretty and feminine in a provocative way. 'Her short black hair was brushed into an upward curl at the ends, and on it she wore a jaunty black and red beret, tilted on the side of her head.' Her name was Captain Aura Rhanes. Bethurum's wife was at first jealous of her husband's new friend, but apart from one incident when the Captain invited him to touch her to see if she was real, and then had to push him away when he tried to escalate the experiment, their relationship was one of teacher and pupil. In the end Truman Bethurum and his wife joined together in founding a chapel to preach the gospel of the space people, and the site they were inspired to choose turned out to be literally a gold mine, adding material wealth to the Bethurum's spiritual treasure.

This final incident of the buried treasure, whose existence is indicated by supernatural means, is just one of the many archaic themes which the stories of these American space visionaries provide. In Menger's case they are obvious and presumably unconscious. There is the magic round table, the tree marking the spot where the space visions appear (a feature of the Fatima miracle, the Joan of Arc story and countless others) and above all the Lady of the Rock herself, in many ways reminiscent of the pre-Christian local deities, goddesses such as the 'mouras encantadas' of Portugal who in the form of beautiful women with the tails of serpents haunted the rocks, caves and lonely places of the countryside. Their legend and that of their relations the mermaids, survived side by side with the cult of the Virgin Mary to which they contributed, making a dramatic reappearance at Fatima in 1917. Also identical with the Fatima incident is the appearance of the flying saucer in which the Lady of the Rock visited Menger for the second time; spinning, pulsating, changing colour as it approached the earth like the sun coming down from the sky, this is exactly how the vehicle of the Lady of Fatima was at the time described. Menger's girls, too, are more mermaid than woman; provocative but chaste, their long blonde tresses floating in the breeze, they may leave their own element for a time to flirt with men, but must ultimately remain elusive and unattainable. The period evoked is above all that of Arthurian legend, the Knight sent into the world to shed light in the darkness and win the favours of a beautiful woman. The Holy Grail appears, both in Menger's vision of the radiant flying saucer and explicitly in the work of another space visionary, Orfeo Angelucci, author of *The Secret of the Saucers*, who on one occasion found on the bumper of his car a clear translucent

95

crystal cup left for him by his celestial visitors.

The contribution which these stories make to the study of the physical aspect of flying saucers is negligible, although they can seem highly relevant to the problem as a whole if approached in the right way, not in a negative spirit of weighing belief with disbelief, but with the humility that respects other people's ways of expressing themselves. The objects in the sky, which began to be reported in the late 1940s, have a meaning far beyond the merely physical. As we have just seen they inspired the whole literary tradition of the Adamski school. Their appearance gave rise to the naïve but earnest space philosophy, a sort of codifying of a mixture of enlightened modern beliefs, popular superstition and folklore. There are elements of vegetarianism, eastern philosophy, a messianic cult and the folklore of technology all fused together by the catalyst of flying saucers. It may be said that this was the first popular attempt to develop a way of thought for the new age. The flying saucer phenomenon may be seen as a stimulus, possibly deliberately inspired, to the evolution of a new system following the eclipse of the old. The Christian era, during which so much former knowledge was suppressed or distorted, is now reaching the end of its two thousand years span. The reappearance today of so many pre-Christian beliefs and images may be a sign that the events of the past on which they were based are about to be repeated. The coming of flying saucers is both a part of these events and a portent of the changes which their coming will bring.

CHAPTER SIX

Disappearing People

Ay, though we hunted high and low
And hunted everywhere,
Of the three men's fate we found no trace
Of any kind in any place
But a door ajar and an untouched meal
And an overtoppled chair.

And as we listened in the gloom
Of that forsaken living-room—
A chill clutch on our breath—
We thought how ill-chance came to all
Who kept the Flannan Light,
And how the rock had been the death
Of many a likely lad—
How six had come to a sudden end
And three had gone stark mad,
And one, whom we'd all known as friend,
Had leapt from the lantern one still night
And fallen dead by the lighthouse wall—
And long we thought
Of the three we sought
And on what might yet befall.

Like curs a glance has brought to heel
We listened, flinching there,
And looked and looked on the untouched meal
And the overtoppled chair.

We seemed to stand for an endless while,
Though still no word was said,

Three men alive on Flannan Isle
Who thought on three men dead.

From *Flannan Isle* by Wilfrid Wilson Gibson

No less terrifying than the possibility of alien creatures in our midst is the belief that people can be abducted from earth. This is another of those persistent fears which existed at all times in the past and have recently reappeared as a part of the flying saucer legend. Every day, we are told, twenty people in Britain leave their homes and vanish. In most cases, obviously there is a simple explanation. But sometimes a man disappears in circumstances so strange that it does indeed look as if he has left the face of the earth. The remarkable American, Charles Fort, spent years of his life collecting, arranging and analysing reports of such occurrences. From newspaper cuttings he built up a fantastic collection of mysterious and unexplained events. These included reports of strange things falling from the sky, the appearance of unidentified flying objects, showers of frogs and various animals, 'teleportations' (people or objects suddenly snatched away from one place and set down in another), all the varied, odd phenomena, which because they fall within the province of no known science, are never properly investigated. One of his studies was that of missing people.

Fort recorded many disappearances. Sherman Church of Michigan, who vanished for ever on entering a mill, although the building was demolished in the search for him; Isaac Martin, who on 23 April 1885 suddenly dematerialised in the middle of a field where he was working; the thirteen children of Cork who mysteriously vanished in August 1869. In 1924 there was the strange case of the two RAF officers, Day and Stewart, whose aeroplane crashed in the Iraq desert. Their footsteps were traced in the sand away from the wreck into the desert until suddenly they came to an end. The two men had apparently vanished into the air.

Then there are the cases of teleportation. The most remarkable is the story uncovered by the late M. K. Jessup and included in his book *The Case for the UFOs*.

On 25 October 1593 a Spanish soldier suddenly found himself in the main square of Mexico City. Since he was unable to explain how he came to be there, and since the uniform he was wearing was that of a regiment stationed across the Pacific in the Philippine Islands, the soldier was arrested and tried by the Inquisition. All he could say was that he had been on duty the previous day, 24 October, in Manila, the capital of the Philippines, 9,000 miles away. At that time the journey would have taken almost a year, but the soldier claimed that he had been transported from one spot to another 'in less time than it takes for a cock to crow'. He gave precise details of his life in Manila up to the time when he left, and informed his interrogators that the Spanish governor of the Philippines had recently been killed. Many months later, the soldier's story was confirmed when news of the governor's death arrived from Manila, together with other evidence which made it plain that the soldier had indeed been transported across the Pacific in the course of a single day.

The traditional solution to an unexplained case of teleportation and people disappearing is that they are the work of some unearthly agency, the form of which varies according to the popular myth of the time. Today this agency is often believed to be connected with the phenomenon of flying saucers, and there are actual reports of beings from these craft kidnapping people. An account appeared in 1965 in the *Flying Saucer Review* of how the previous year a number of people were attacked in Venezuela by some small creatures from a flying saucer who clawed at them and attempted to drag them into their vessel. And on one occasion it was the mysterious flying objects themselves who abducted a man. The victim, a Brazilian called Mafra, was swallowed up in a cloud of swirling dust or gas emitted by two globe-like objects which had landed outside his house. His son, Raimundo, saw his father disappear, and told investigators how, the night before, both of them had been terrified by shadowy figures creeping about their bedroom. The reputation, which flying saucers have acquired, has provided the most sinister side to their legend.

This belief, that abductions are carried out by an unearthly race, represents a return, after many centuries of vague superstitious speculation, to the days when the nature of the gods was generally known. The flying saucer legend is, as will be seen later, essentially the same as that which inspired worship in the past, and the forms of this worship were based on the known practice of the gods of landing on hilltops to take men away from the earth. Today it is not only individuals who are abducted, but ships, aeroplanes and small, isolated groups. And in many cases in recent years, where this has happened the old belief in the kidnappers from the sky has been revived as an explanation. Writers such as M. K. Jessup and Major Donald Keyhoe, who have re-examined old mysteries and investigated recent disappearances, have concluded that there may be some force from outer space responsible for them.

Jessup in his book *The Case for the UFOs* gave several instances where, he believed, an extra-terrestrial agency has been the cause of people and objects mysteriously vanishing. One case which he cited was the classical mystery of the 'Marie Celeste'. The story is so often repeated and is so remarkable that people sometimes think that the 'Marie Celeste' never really existed. But the facts are indisputable. The 'Marie Celeste' was a small brig seen at Christmas 1872 sailing in mid Atlantic with no one on board. The ship which found her, the British brig 'Dei Gratia', had noticed something erratic in her course, and had sent a party to board her. The 'Marie Celeste' appeared to be in perfect order. Her cargo was intact and she was undamaged by storms. Nothing was missing from the ship except the crew and of them no trace was ever found. According to the men from the 'Dei Gratia' who boarded her, the 'Marie Celeste' had only just been abandoned. Breakfast was laid in the cabin, and three men had evidently been disturbed during their meal, for their plates were half empty and their cups of tea still slightly warm. The galley stove had been raked out but was still quite hot, and on it was set a saucepan with a nicely boiled chicken. Pipes and tobacco and a few sheets of paper lay about the cabin in confusion.

The derelict ship was taken into Gibraltar where her appearance caused great excitement. An inquiry was held, but no reasonable theory which could account for the absence of the crew was ever put forward. There was no reason why they should have abandoned the ship, which bore no signs of having been in trouble. It is hard to imagine any accident which might have removed them all without leaving any clue to its nature, and they could hardly have been abducted by human agency without some sort of struggle of which there was no sign. It is not therefore surprising that the mystery of the 'Marie Celeste' has been so often taken as an example of the workings of the supernatural. Jessup, writing in the 1950s, when the flood of modern flying saucer reports was first appearing, was able to apply the revived belief in visitors from outer space to the problem of the 'Marie Celeste', and in doing so provided perhaps the most plausible theory yet to explain the disappearance of her crew.

Besides the various cases where ships or their crews have unaccountably vanished, Jessup described other strange occurrences. There was the story of Joe La Belle, a trapper in northern Canada who, in November 1930 entered an Eskimo village to find no sign of any inhabitants. The caribou skin tents were undamaged and contained all the possessions of an Eskimo tribe, clothing, cooking pots and rifles. Evidently the camp had not been willingly abandoned, nor had its inhabitants gone off on a hunting trip, since the rifles they would have taken with them were left behind. So were the dogs. The trapper found seven of them lying dead all together just outside the village. For some reason they had left the camp and had starved to death in a group. Not only were the living inhabitants of the village missing; a grave covered by a cairn of stones had been opened, the stones piled neatly on one side, and there was no sign of a body. A police investigation found no trace of the missing Eskimos and no clue to why the village was abandoned. Another Arctic mystery on a much larger scale was the disappearance during the fourteenth century of the entire population of the Norse colony of Greenland. Trade between the colony and Europe had declined and for some hundred years no ships had called there. When finally a mission to Greenland was dispatched, no trace of the colonists, once about 10,000, was found. An investigation of some of the settlements showed that the departure of their inhabitants had been sudden. But there was never any satisfactory natural explanation how or why it took place.

Curiously enough, Jessup himself died in rather mysterious circumstances. Some were led by this to remember the legend that people who occupy themselves with the study of the supernatural are liable to meet an untimely fate. Here again an old belief has been revived in the flying saucer legend. A book by Gray Barker, published some years ago in America, gave examples of people who have been in various ways discouraged from pursuing their investigations into the flying saucer question. One of these was Albert K. Bender, head of an organisation called the International Flying Saucer Bureau. Suddenly in 1953, when the Bureau was well established and successful, Bender closed it down. Some ten years later he published a book, *Flying Saucers and the Three Men* in which he claimed that three men had visited him and frightened him to such an extent that he had wanted nothing more to do with the subject of flying saucers. Recently it has been said that certain other writers on this subject have suffered the mishaps which traditionally come to those who concern themselves too closely with the supernatural. In the past it was the practitioners of black magic who put themselves in danger, especially if, like Faust, they used their illicit knowledge for personal gain. Any enquiry into the ways of supernatural creatures was thought to be unwise. People who became too interested in fairies and the like were liable to vanish, if not bodily at least in spirit. It was believed that something of the sort happened to Robert Kirk, minister of the church at Aberfoyle at the end of the seventeenth century. Kirk, an excellent Gaelic scholar, spent a lifetime inquiring into accounts of hauntings by ghosts and fairies among the local people. His findings, in which he included the opinion that fairies were made of 'congealed air', were published in a book called, *The Secret Commonwealth; or an Essay on the Nature and Actions of the Subterranean (and for the most part) Invisible People heretofor going under the names of Faunes and Fairies, or the lyke, among the Low country Scots, as they are described by those who have the second sight.* His obsession gave him a somewhat sinister reputation, stimulated by the manner of his death. He collapsed and died on a fairy hill, a little grassy mound traditionally a haunt of the fairy race. People said that he had not died naturally, but that his spirit had been captured by the fairies. This belief was later expressed by Sir Walter Scott in his poem *The Lady of the Lake.*

'*It was between the night and day,*
 When the Fairy King has power,
 That I sank down in a sinful fray,
 And 'twixt life and death was snatch'd away
 To the joyless Elfin bower.'

Stories such as this, involving the supernatural, became increasingly popular during the nineteenth century. The rationalism of the age had destroyed the old concepts of the forms which supernatural creatures assumed. Men were said to be unique in the universe, the sole intelligent creation. But, although suppressed, the belief in a supernatural race persisted, finding its expression in the romantic literature of the time. Even though the possibility of extra-terrestrial life was hardly suggested, nineteenth-century writers were quite willing to imply that certain mysterious events were brought about by some unearthly power. The disappearance in 1809 of the diplomat Benjamin Bathurst, who outside an inn 'stepped round to the horses' heads and was never seen again', was said by some to be the work of the Devil. So was that of Owen Parfitt forty years earlier. The popular explanation of the fate of this evil old man, who suddenly vanished one summer afternoon while sitting on a chair in front of his house in Shepton Mallet immobilised by a stroke and within sight of several people was given by Southey.

> *'The Devil he passed a cottage trim*
> *A cottage cosy and trim,*
> *And he said with a grin*
> *"I'll just step in,*
> *For I think there's somebody here*
> *That's been in my debt for many a year".'*

This vague belief in a supernatural force capable of removing people from earth still survives. It appears in an account by Oliver Stewart in his book, *Danger in the Air*, of how a modern Avro Tudor aeroplane 'Star Ariel' vanished during a short flight in perfect weather near Bermuda in 1949. Stewart, who considered this to be the greatest mystery of aviation, wrote,

> 'A large aeroplane disappeared and left no trace. In the past the disappearance of ships at sea has sometimes given rise to legends and strange beliefs. This does not happen with aircraft, for they are the products of an age which does not believe in such stories.'

A far more committed writer than Oliver Stewart on the subject of disappearing aircraft is Major Donald Keyhoe, late of the US Marines. Keyhoe has written a number of books on flying saucers including one *The Flying Saucer Conspiracy* which first led C. G. Jung to take an interest in the subject. In this book Keyhoe explores a possible link between the appearance of flying saucers and the various inexplicable cases where aircraft have vanished without trace. His most striking example was the complete disappearance on 5 December 1945 of six aircraft and their crews.

On that day five modern Air Force Avengers took off on a short routine flight of two hours. Each aeroplane carried a crew of three, and had been found to be in perfect order in every way. Ninety minutes later something odd happened. What it was was never discovered, but all five pilots appeared to lose all sense of where they were. Their radio signals became more confused, and the flight leader in a panic was heard to resign his command to another pilot. At this a huge Martin Mariner sea plane, fully equipped with rescue gear and with a crew of thirteen on board, was sent to find out what was wrong. Neither the sea plane nor the five Avengers were ever heard of again. The Navy and Air Force carried out the biggest search operation ever undertaken, covering an area of 280,000 square miles. Every bit of debris spotted in the sea or on the beaches from Florida to the Bahamas was examined, but there was no clue. A Naval court of inquiry was unable to arrive at any conclusion about the fate of the six aircraft.

Keyhoe seriously suggests that the aeroplanes and their crews were somehow abducted by an extra-terrestrial force, and, when taken together with other similar occurrences this suggestion does not seem altogether fantastic. But even if the disappearance of these aircraft was somehow connected with the phenomenon of flying saucers, the true nature of these objects is no nearer to being resolved. Although the reality of the visions in the sky can now hardly be denied and certain governments are already deeply concerned about their appearance, the enormous impact which their coming must produce has not yet begun to make itself felt. It is clear that they do not originate from anywhere on earth, yet there is a surprising reluctance on the part of almost everyone to consider the revolutionary changes which our positive identification of extra-terrestrial life must bring. Lenin had thought about the subject, for he said in conversation with H. G. Wells,

'All human conceptions are on the scale of our planet. They are based on the pretension that the technical potential, although it will develop, will never exceed the "terrestrial limit". If we succeed in establishing interplanetary communications, all our philosophical, moral and social views will have to be revised.'

Unfortunately there is little immediate chance that a general consensus of opinion will allow our attitudes to be revised in any particular direction. We seem destined to undergo a period of chaos in

104

which a resurgence of old beliefs will struggle with our present out-worn system of nineteenth-century logic until such time as a new orthodoxy can emerge. A sign that this period is about to begin is our growing obsession with the 'legends and strange beliefs' mentioned by Oliver Stewart. And it may be a hopeful sign that already some sort of pattern, by which these things may be interpreted, seems to be available. This pattern can be seen in the way that the study of 'occult' or abnormal phenomena is increasingly revolving round the legend of flying saucers. Our conscious awakening to the UFO problem opens the way to the study of many subjects which have no place in orthodox science. This is how the problem of disappearing people and objects came to be connected with that of flying saucers.

What is more, it seems as if the link between the two subjects is far older than is generally realised. The disappearance of people from the earth and their transference to another world is a popular theme in folklore. Men are snatched away to a land in the sky, or they wandered into a cave and enter an enchanted fairy world where they are kept for many years. In every case they enter into a different dimension where the ordinary rules of time do not apply. The most significant form in which this story appears is in the Welsh versions, which differ from each other only in detail.

The outline of the story is that two men are walking together through the fields, when they see a fairy ring in the grass. This is one of those mysterious circles of coarse grass and fungus, the cause of which has never been explained, but which are traditionally said to be the rings in which fairies dance. One of the men steps inside the ring, and is immediately whirled away out of sight, swept up in a fairy dance. The other man rushes home and describes what has happened, but his story is not believed, and suspicion falls upon him of having somehow done away with his friend. In some versions, after consulting a wise man, he is able to recapture his friend by returning to the circle on the anniversary of the disappearance and dragging him out as he dances by. But a more horrifying ending is the one where the man does not return for a hundred years or so. However long he has been away, and this is a feature of all such stories, he thinks his absence was only for a few minutes. The man who has spent many years in the other world goes back to his farm, and is surprised to find it occupied by strangers. During the ex-planations which follow, some old woman is found who remembers the tale of the man who vanished in the fairy ring, or the story is discovered in parish records. In any case the man is given something to eat, but when he touches food he crumbles to dust.

This point is emphasised in most of the stories which have a man returning to earth after years in an alien world. As long as he refrains from some ordinary human action, which varies from story to story, he appears to be the same as when he went away. But when the spell is broken, he ages, disintegrates and dies. Frequently this is caused by the man taking food or drink; but sometimes the action of setting foot on the ground is fatal. Ossian, the Irish hero, was taken as lover by the Queen of Tirnan Og, the fairy country of perpetual youth. For years he led an ideal existence in the palace gardens with his beautiful wife, until one day he did the one thing he had been told not to do. In all the Garden of Eden legends one thing is forbidden, and it is precisely this that the hero can never finally refrain from doing. In this case Ossian stepped onto a forbidden stone, and immediately felt a longing to return to earth. The Queen let him go but with a warning not to dismount from his horse or in any way touch the earth. This proved too much for him and while helping a man he met to pick up a sack from the ground, Ossian dismounted and immediately shrivelled up into a feeble old man.

The main feature common to all stories where the hero travels to an unearthly land is the distortion of the time scale. Men who think they have been away for a few minutes, find on their return to earth that years have elapsed. As long as they remain within the influence of the supernatural world they do not age, nor do they notice the passing of time. But when they return to earth, they find that the time they have spent away has counted against them, and that the years which seemed as minutes are for ever lost. In many cases they do not live long to enjoy the sensation that their reappearance has caused, their first attempt at resuming an earthly existence bringing about their death.

It is interesting to find in these stories, which are of great antiquity, a recognition of the relativity of time. E. S. Hartland in *The Science of Fairy Stories* suggests that the horrifying detail of the man returning from fairyland to find everything changed was emphasised and exaggerated by the early Christian church as a warning against having anything to do with supernatural beings. Certainly the Church tried to suppress or christianise all descriptions of dealings with creatures

106

of another world, and the persistence of this story is proof of the hold it must have had on popular imagination. It is not therefore surprising that such stories are reappearing in modern form today. In the story of the Indian hunter and the maidens from the sky, given in an earlier chapter, the ring on the grass marked the spot where the circular sky vehicle had landed. The fairy ring in the Welsh tale was also the place from which the man disappeared, whirled up into the sky. Both these stories have something in common with those told today where a ring of crushed, burnt or discoloured grass marks the spot from which a flying saucer has been seen to take off. Concerning the different scale of time, we know now what could hardly have been known in the remote past, that this may vary in other parts of the universe. A man from earth taken into outer space may return at a point in time quite different from where he left. Maybe, as Fort suggests on the evidence of apparently anachronistic people who have from time to time appeared on earth, something of the sort has already happened. People may have been abducted, kept for a time in another dimension, which from the incomprehensibly higher culture of its inhabitants seems to them a sort of paradise, and then returned to earth. One could see this as part of a scientific experiment, an attempt to preserve people in space during years of devastation on earth, to transfer them from one planet or time dimension to another, to breed them with other, extra-terrestrial races. If this is so, the experiments which legends describe are those that have failed. Human life, which can be artificially adapted to existence outside the earth, has not yet been able to survive replanting.

Not all the evidence of popular belief points to this conclusion. A very persistent story is that certain individuals, chosen for their outstanding personal qualities, are being kept in a kind of limbo against the day when they will be needed on earth again. King Arthur is perhaps the best known example. From all over Britain and other parts of Europe come stories of how he never died, but rests with his band of heroes by the round table (a representation of the sky vehicle), waiting for a second birth. A great many other heroes have the same reputation. King Wenzel sleeps under the Blanik mountain of Bohemia, Barbarossa beneath a mountain in Thuringia. Others live in the sky. Ogier the Dane, one of the Paladins of Charlemagne, is reputed already to have made one reappearance. On his death he was taken to the supernatural land, Avalon, by the immortal Morgan the

Fay, and lived with her for two hundred years. Their life of ideal happiness was interrupted when France was in need of a saviour, and Ogier with a magic ring and torch went down to her aid. His task accomplished, he returned to Avalon, where like Arthur, he lives still.

Naturally no one would argue that myths such as these contain much in the way of detailed historical truth. In the same way no sensible man would seriously claim that the disappearance of Benjamin Bathurst, or the crew of the 'Mary Celeste', and the death of Robert Kirk were *beyond any doubt* caused by forces other than natural and known ones. Yet the very fact that, where any obvious natural explanation seems to be lacking, people are liable, almost eager, to speculate in terms of the supernatural, has in itself some significance. This is particularly the case where these speculations all lead in the same direction and towards one conclusion, towards the ancient belief, based in the past on actual first-hand knowledge, that people and objects can be physically removed from earth by an intelligent force of which we are not at present consciously aware. The remnants of this belief, retained in the unconscious mind as a kind of half-heard rumour, have survived to the present day partly in christianised forms of old histories, partly through repeated incidents where abductions from the earth have apparently taken place again, and are now merging with the recently observed flying saucer phenomenon to produce a new attitude towards the universe, not unlike that held in the remote pre-Christian, pre-Sophoclean ages.

What we now suspect was in the past openly known. The 'gods demand sacrifices, perfect specimens for their own scientific purposes. In the days when the nature of the gods was known, their desires studied, and the benefits they could bring enjoyed, sacrifices were left for them on the high places which they frequented. The relationship between the gods of mythology and the superior race from the sky, to whom the first sacrifices were made, is a large subject which must soon be studied in detail. What we do know is that sacrifices were made to the gods, a practice which survived into historical times in the barbaric mass human sacrifices of later degenerate cultures. These pointless orgies were performed through a debased memory of times when an open knowledge of the gods was the centre of men's lives.

The human specimens which were offered to the gods were the best of the race as the 'lamb without blemish, a male of the first year' of the first Passover. They were taken to an appointed place, a place whose reputation for sanctity has frequently survived to this day. Such places were on the tops of hills or on islands. Here they were left for the gods to remove.

To be chosen as a sacrifice was an honour to which only heroes aspired, and, in early days at least, no one suffered this fate unwillingly. Whoever was taken was supposed to be spared an ordinary death, and to live for ever with the gods as an immortal. The list of heroes who were removed from earth in this way is a long one. Oedipus in his old age was caught up into the sky from a high spot outside Athens; Romulus was taken up in a chariot of fire as, of course, was Elijah, in both cases from a holy place outside a city. The detail of the fiery chariot descending and removing the sacrifice is a very precise memory of what actually happened. Both Hercules and Moses ascended bodily into the sky from a mountain top; the Welsh hero, Llew Llaw Gyffes, disappeared from a high place in the form of an eagle, and the hero of British mythology, Robin Hood, met his end in the top of a tower.

The break in open co-operation between the gods and men, brought about by the sudden advance in human civilisation which this alliance had produced, meant the end of the original practice of human sacrifice. But the confusion and terror which followed the departure of the gods, the rise of superstition and the decline of culture led to the practice being continued in the appalling mass slaughter of sacrificial victims by priests anxious to enter again into communication with the superior race. Even in those degenerate times many races kept a certain knowledge of astronomy and of the nature of the gods, although it was but a perverted form of what had been known in the days of open communication, and it was these races who most developed an obsession with mass sacrifice. The Druids, according to Caesar, filled wickerwork giants with men and women, and set fire to them; the Irish slaughtered a large percentage of their population to the golden idol, Cromm Cruagh, later destroyed by St Patrick; the Aztecs killed untold numbers of people on the artificial high places, the flat-topped pyramids of Mexico.

The gods had departed, but the places they had appointed for sacrifice remained, and were still held in awe. To this day they are remembered, the high places, hill and mountain tops, haunted by spirits. Where there was no suitable natural elevation on which they could land, an artificial one was built. This took the form either of an elevated platform, a pyramid, examples of which occur in the Middle East, in Mexico and in the islands of the South Seas, or perhaps even of a tower. A great mystery surrounds the occurrence of vast numbers of round towers in many parts of the world and the use to which they were put. There are the duns and brochs of Scotland, the slender Irish towers, the early East Anglian round towers which were later incorporated into church buildings. In Sardinia are thousands of identical towers, the nuraghi, the purpose of which is lost; only the Parsees retain some tradition of the original use of their towers. The 'dakhma' or tower of silence is a circular building placed on elevated ground. Bodies of the dead are exposed on its summit to be eaten by birds. In this way the dead disappear entirely into the air.

It may well be that the memory behind this practice is of a time when the tops of towers, like hilltops natural and artificial, were used for exposing the sacrifices offered to the gods. A remarkable piece of evidence that something of the sort may have happened is to be found in the 'vitrified forts' of Scotland. These round towers usually built on high ground have at some period of their existence been subjected to a heat so great that some of the stones of which they are built have actually melted and run together to form a solid concrete block. Moreover the heat must have been applied from a position directly above the towers, for it is always the stones at the top which have been vitrified and never the foundations. Some writers such as Desmond Leslie, who have noticed the mystery of vitrified towers, have suggested that the stones were melted by an object in the sky, hovering above the tops of the towers and directing upon them a fierce blast of heat. It would hardly seem possible, in this case, that a human being could have then been taken from the top of the tower alive. On the other hand a fiery chariot or flame-breathing dragon are frequently mentioned in mythological accounts of a man being taken up into the sky. The question of whether people ever were actually taken away from the tops of towers or whether towers were built for later imitative and ritual sacrifice is uncertain. Certainly they are all much later than the pyramids and artificial mounds which were built for true sacrificial purposes. Yet whatever their eventual use – and they were frequently used as watchtowers, fortresses and churches after their original purpose had lapsed – their similarity to each other and the way they are distributed suggests only one reason for their construction, as platforms for the exposure of sacrifices to the sky gods. This would also explain the number of heroes and legendary figures – Merlin, Robin Hood and Bishop Hatto are examples – who met their ends in towers.

The position with artificial mounds and sacred hills is more certain. There can be little doubt that they were the scenes of sacrifices to and landings by beings from the sky. A feature of many of them is that they stand above and are connected by a path to a stone circle or the site of a pre-Christian temple. Croagh Patrick in County Mayo, the mountain from which St Patrick ejected the snakes, is an example. Another is Silbury Hill, the greatest artificial mound in Europe, which stands near the Stone Age cathedral, Avebury. Silbury, which so impressed King Charles that he demanded of the antiquarian Aubrey an immediate and exhaustive report on it, is evidently not a place of burial, as has been suggested, since excavations, including a shaft sunk from the top to ground level have always failed to find any evidence for this. From its circular flattened top it was evidently a place of sacrifice.

The stone circles which were laid out at the foot of sacrificial hills, were temples where the human offerings to the gods were consecrated before being led up to the summit. There still remain a considerable number of sites where this relationship between hilltop and stone circle can be demonstrated, and a great many more where the site of the pre-Christian temple is now occupied by a church. This is probably the case with Uffington Church in Berkshire, standing below the heights of the White Horse which were once among the most sacred in Britain. Another temple site, a raised circular mound now incorporated in a modern graveyard, can be found in the valley below the elevated vitrified tower just west of Dingwall in Scotland. Arbor Low in Derbyshire has an avenue leading to an artificial eminence, and there are many other examples on Salisbury Plain and other parts of the country besides those at Avebury and County Mayo, already mentioned.

One of the first to recognise something of the significance of the avenues which lead from some stone circles was the great eighteenth-century figure Dr William Stukely, described by a contemporary as 'a learned and honest man', and a mixture of 'simplicity, drollery, absurdity, ingenuity, superstition, and antiquarianism'. Stukely became obsessed by the idea of the Druids, attributed to them many of the prehistoric monuments of England, and established a new

111

Fig. 3 *The greatest artificial mound in Europe, Silbury Hill*

druidic order with himself as 'Chyndonax' the Arch-Druid. In his
garden at Grantham he laid out a Druid temple and grove with an old
mistletoe-covered apple tree in the centre. All this has not endeared
him to modern archæologists, whose furious rejection of any
theories involving Druids seems almost pathological. While paying
tribute to Stukely's early antiquarian observations, they have suppressed the startling conclusions to which he came over the true
meaning of many of the stone circles and avenues of Britain. Indeed
in a recent biography they are only referred to obliquely and with
scorn.

Stukely claimed that, seen from the air, the pattern of prehistoric
Britain became plain. The circles and avenues were huge representations of serpents and indicated a serpent-worshipping religion
which looked to the sky for its gods. The meaning of the serpent
symbol, its identification with the sky vehicle, has already been discussed. Recent evidence has shown that much of Stukely's work which
has been dismissed as lies was in fact accurate at the time he wrote;
stones, which were standing in his time, have since been removed,
earthworks ploughed up and the like. What is interesting is that
several of the places which Stukely mentions as scenes of the cult

of the serpent from the sky, are places to which legends and rumours of sacrifices and disappearing people still attach. One of these is Callernish, the great stone circle of the serpent and winged disc on the west coast of Lewis in the Outer Hebrides.

The approach to Callernish is a dramatic experience. It stands high up just outside a small crofting village surrounded on three sides by arms of the sea. From it are visible three other stone circles on neighbouring headlands, and others are to be found in the same area. At midsummer the light never entirely fades and the pale sea below is visible all night, dotted with small dark islands, each with their heroic legend. The cyclopean ruins and atmosphere of past greatness which the now deserted country pervades have the same spirit as the Greek islands, and reveal the Callernish district as a centre of important activity in the past.

Callernish is unusual among temples of its sort as having no hill or mound associated with it. Yet it is obviously one of those places from which sacrifices were taken off to the spot where the gods received them. The key to the mystery can be found in the Flannan Islands, a fearfully remote group of small islets situated in the Atlantic Ocean some miles off the west coast of Lewis opposite Callernish.

Of all the holy islands round the coasts of Scotland the Flannans must have been the most awesome. Martin, the Scottish antiquarian who travelled in the Hebrides in the last years of the seventeenth century, once asked a native of Lewis who had been to the Flannans whether he prayed at home as fervently as he did on the islands. The man 'plainly confessed that he did not: adding further, that these remote islands were places of inherent sanctity; and that there was none ever yet landed in them but found himself more disposed to devotion there, than anywhere else'. The alternative name for the islands, the Seven Hunters, is another indication of their magic reputation, for a group of seven islands – and there are about twenty rocks and islets in the Flannan group – often stands in fairy stories for the islands of paradise, islands such as the seven islands of Wak, which Hasan, the hero of an Arabian Nights Story, visited in search of his swan-maiden bride.

Martin also has a curious description of the rituals which Lewismen carried out whenever they visited the Flannan Islands. Every summer a boat went out to the islands to collect sea-birds and their eggs and to leave sheep to graze on the rich grass which grows there. Any man who had not been there before had to be accompanied by another to show him what to do. After the voyage and the landing, both of which involved the observance of a complicated series of rites and taboos, the men approached the tiny ruined chapel, the only building on the islands, and taking off their jackets and shirts prayed according to established precedent, approaching the chapel on their knees, and later processing round it in a clockwise direction. Other customs had to be observed. No bird must be killed with a stone or after evening worship. No sheep suet must ever be removed from the islands. Most extraordinary of all, the men had to speak in a different dialect to that which they used at home. Certain things were called by different names, as if the memory of a long vanished language was being perpetuated. Words never used elsewhere were kept for the annual visit to the Flannan Islands.

Who built the chapel which stands on the largest island is not known, but its existence emphasises the sanctity of the place. Evidently the islands were thought of as a kind of other world, haunted by supernatural creatures and the spirits of the dead. Probably like Heligoland or the Scilly Islands, also in the extreme west, which are covered with a vast number of burial mounds, the Flannan Islands were the islands of the dead, the place to which people were ferried and never returned. This would explain their extreme holiness and their baleful character. It might also shed some light on something which happened there early this century, one of the great unsolved mysteries of modern times.

In the nineteenth century the Flannan Islands had become a problem. Situated on the shipping route to the north of Scotland, their isolated rocks had brought about a number of shipwrecks, any survivors of which had lingered for a time on their bleak surfaces before dying of hunger or exposure. It was therefore decided to place a lighthouse on the largest of the group, Eilean Mor, to be maintained by a staff of four men. With great difficulty the undertaking was completed and in December 1899 the first light shone out from the Flannan Islands. The tower, seventy-five feet high, stood near the old chapel. Every fortnight a boat from Breascleat, the next village to Callernish, went out to the islands, as it does today, to bring supplies and to take off one of the keepers for his period of leave. He would return after a fortnight and the next in turn would be relieved.

114

On 26 December 1900 the Lighthouse Board's ship 'Hesperus' approached the Flannan Islands with Joseph Moore, the Keeper who was returning from leave. A signal was hoisted, but there was no reply from the lighthouse where three men, James Ducat, Thomas Marshall and Donald McArthur, should have been on duty. A small boat was dispatched to the landing stage and Moore scrambled ashore and made his way to the tower. It was deserted. The fire was out, the clock had stopped, and the light was extinguished. A frantic search was made of the island, but with no result. The three men were nowhere to be found.

The first solution which sprang to mind was obviously that the three men had been swept into the sea by a storm. One of the landing stages, some hundred feet below the central plateau of the island showed signs of damage, and it was known that a violent gale had blown on 12 and 13 December which had presumably caused the island to be battered by high waves. Yet this solution was soon found to be impossible. The Keepers' log book was completed up to the morning of the 15th, so the men had presumably vanished some time during that day, but from 14 to 19 December the sea had been comparatively calm, the gale having abated. In any case, Moore, who naturally knew how matters were conducted at the lighthouse, said that it was inconceivable for any man to go down to the landing in rough weather let alone all three keepers together.

So the matter rested. How the three men could disappear from the Flannan Islands on a calm day is a question which has never been answered. In a case like this when there appears to be no obvious natural solution, it was only to be expected that people should look for a more sinister cause for the tragedy. After all, at the time when it took place sacrifices were still being made on the island and hillsides of Loch Maree and probably in other remote parts of the Highlands. Stories were put about of pirates and sea monsters, and the reputation of the Flannan Islands as the haunt of spirits was not forgotten. The experience of John Morisone, who had been marooned on the largest of the group in the seventeenth century, was recalled. During his stay he allowed his fire to go out, and had no means of relighting it. He was in despair, for without a fire he seemed certain to perish, when he was suddenly confronted by a man. Without explaining who he was, the man told John Morisone to look for fire on the altar of the chapel. On the altar a flame was burning, and John Morisone was able to light a fire from it and to preserve himself until he was relieved.

Many of the islands to the west of Lewis, of which the Flannans are the most remote, were said to have been the haunt of a supernatural race of small people. Dean Munro, an earlier traveller to the isles, saw some of their tiny bones being dug out of the earth, and himself discovered a skull. There are a number of other records of the existence of this race, and of the hatred and fear which the early Christian Church had of them. There were many contests between the two sides.

St Cuthbert in the seventh century had to drive a pack of demons off Farne Island before he could build his house there. He was armed only with 'The helmet of salvation, the shield of faith and the sword of the spirit which is the word of God'.

St Patrick evicted a race of small men from the Isle of Man. They returned later in the form of the fairies.

Sometimes the little people struck back. St Guthlac was tormented by them on an island in the fens, and on Lewis the inhabitants of the Isle of Pygmies caught a hostile Christian, St Frangus, and hanged him on a hill top.

A theory that MacRitchie and others have made popular is that the little people were the remains of an aboriginal Pictish race, surviving in remote places into comparatively recent times. There may be some truth in this, though why the word of God should have been denied them, and only used to drive them away is hard to say. But the theory does not explain how this little race has continued to appear at all times up to this century. A woman, who only died a few years ago, has described how she spent a night with them.

Mary MacPhee lived on Great Bernera, an island on the west coast of Lewis between the Flannans and the Long Island. When she was four years old, wandering on the hillside opposite her house, she met some little people dressed in green. They took her to a big house and all night she watched them piping and dancing. In the morning they took her to the door of the house and showed her her father's croft on the opposite slope. She set off home down the hill.

All night long her parents and neighbours had been looking for her. Heavy rain had been falling and they were all soaked, but the little girl came down the hill with dry clothes. It was this together with her feeling of warmth and happiness after a night, when everyone had thought she must die of exposure, that convinced them that her story was true.

What is plain from all this is the way in which many islands off the coast of Britain have been haunted by a little race of supernatural beings, none more so than those of the extreme west beyond Lewis, the remotest and most revered of which is the main Flannan Island, Eilean Mor. If this island was the place to which human offerings from Callernish were ferried, it must have been to the little race that the offerings were made. The coming of Christianity meant the end of the sacrifices, and coincided with the departure of the little race itself. Yet, as the Manx tradition says, they came back as fairies and appear to have been seen from time to time up to the present day. Country people were in the habit of leaving food, drink and other offerings for them, a custom which further identifies them with the departed pygmy race to whom sacrifices were made in the past. It is evident that this race of small people, inhabiting the islands of the west, were the pre-Christian gods, and therefore particularly hated by early Christian missionaries. Even after they had ceased to appear openly, the local people retained so much affection for them, that the Christians were for a long time unpopular. Bede tells how the monks at Jarrow, bringing timber down the river Tyne for the construction of their monastery, were swept out to sea on their rafts by a sudden gale, and how the local people mocked them, 'Nobody is going to pray for them. Let not God raise a finger to help them! They have done away with all the old ways of worship and now nobody knows what to do.' Evidently the beginning of the Christian era brought the same sort of uncertainty as is being felt today.

In the light of what we can deduce of the ways of worship and sacrifice of the past, the disappearance of the Flannan Island lighthouse keepers may be seen as an extraordinary repetition of an ancient sacrificial ceremony. The men were taken from the Long Island near Callernish and ferried over to the island of the dead, Eilean Mor, where they were installed in a tower, similar to those once used for human sacrifice, a fine example of which, Dun Carloway, stands on the opposite shore. In the same way as a magic ritual, if properly carried out, may have a predictable result, the sequence of events involved in taking the lighthouse keepers to the Flannan Islands tower ended in their disappearance. The ritual of human sacrifice to the little gods of the western islands was re-enacted, and had the same consequences for the victims as in the days when the great temple of Callernish saw human offerings dispatched to the island of the gods many centuries earlier.

If, as now seems likely, the little men of the islands, whose bones Dean Munro dug up, were of the same 'supernatural' race as the gods who received the human sacrifices from the appointed spot on Eilean Mor, they may also be identified with the modern kidnappers, the 'little green man' who tried to take Mrs Trasco's dog and the abductors of Mr Mafra in Brazil and others. Western Scotland has always been associated with phenomena like those which now form part of the flying saucer legend. Martin tells how 'fiery balls used to follow men in the fields, and spirits like women appear and noises in the air', events not unlike those which the Brazilian farmer in the previous chapter experienced. In the Western Isles the tradition of the little gods from the sky, who took people away with them from certain spots, survived longer than in most other places, and provides a logical link between the old days when people were sacrificed to them and the modern episode of the Flannan Island lighthouse keepers.

But it is not only the Flannans which have retained their reputation into modern times. Mountains and hills, those where offerings to the gods were made, are still considered dangerous and haunted, and occasionally something happens to confirm their reputation. The *Daily Chronicle* of 30 July 1889 contained the following report, quoted by Margaret Barton and Osbert Sitwell in their book *Sober Truth*.

'Constantinople, July 24th.
'The fate of Mr Macmillan is shrouded with mystery. Briefly the circumstances are as follows: Mr Macmillan, who is a son of the well-known publisher, came to Constantinople about three weeks ago on a pleasure-trip. On the 11th inst. he left for Borussa with Mr A. Hardinge, one of the secretaries of the Embassy here. On the 13th, attended by a servant, they started to ride up Mt Olympus. Arrived at the second plateau of the mountain, they dismounted, and after lunching, set out to walk to the summit, leaving the man in charge of the horses. The mountain has two peaks, one higher than the other. After climbing for some distance the travellers separated, Mr Hardinge making for the higher peak, while Mr Mac-

118

millan ascended the lower, with the intention of following his companion afterwards. Arrived at the summit, Mr Hardinge saw Mr Macmillan on the lower cone, and waved his handkerchief to him. Mr Macmillan began the descent, and he was last seen about half-way down the smaller cone. Finding that his friend did not come, Mr Hardinge came down, and went to the place where he had last seen him. There was no trace of Mr Macmillan. He was not to be found, and Mr Hardinge and the servant, after searching in all directions, returned to the town and telegraphed to the British Embassy at Therapia the news of Mr Macmillan's strange disappearance.

'His relatives in England were informed, and telegraphed that no expense was to be spared to find the lost man. Mr Block, dragoman of the Embassy, organised search parties, sending out seventy men in various directions, and offered a reward of £500 for Mr Macmillan living, and £25 for his body. Two hundred men have been engaged in the search. All has been fruitless.

'The man who accompanied the travellers says that he was within earshot of Mr Macmillan all the time, and that when he last saw him he was about half-way down the peak.

'Conjecture is rife as to the fate of Mr Macmillan. There are numbers of Circassians and others who would not hesitate either to kill or carry off any traveller. But they are business-like gentry, and, if they had him alive, would most certainly ere this have named the ransom they demanded. Had he been killed the murderers would probably have "found" the body and claimed the £25. The guides state that there are on the mountain no crevasses or fissures into which a traveller could fall; and even had there been his body must have been discovered by the searchers.'

The authors of *Sober Truth* add, 'No trace was ever found of the missing man, and no satisfactory solution to the mystery has ever been put forward'.

Of all the high places in the world, places of contact between men and gods, none has a greater reputation for sanctity than the mountain from which Mr Macmillan disappeared, Olympus the seat of Zeus, headquarters of the divine race. Other peaks, of which similar stories are told, have claimed modern victims. Everest, the 'white god' of the Himalayas, was the scene of the disappearance in 1924 of

Mallory and Irvine, last seen on the final stage of their climb to the summit. Its haunted reputation is notorious. The semi-mythical creatures said to infest it, the Abominable Snowmen, are believed by the natives to steal people, particularly red-heads, a curious detail since red hair is often a mark of the sacrificial victim in other parts of the world. It is significant that something like a flying saucer sighting from Everest was described by Frank Smyth in his book *Adventures of a Mountaineer*. Smyth was writing of his climb on Everest in 1933.

'I was making my way back towards Camp Six when, chancing to look up, I saw two dark objects floating in the blue sky. In shape they resembled kite balloons, except that one appeared to possess short, squat wings. As they hovered motionless, they seemed to pulsate in and out as though they were breathing. It seemed to me that my brain was working normally, but to test myself I looked away. The objects did not follow my gaze but were still there when I looked back. So I looked away again, but this time identified by name various details of the landscape by way of a mental test. Yet when I again looked back, the objects were still visible. A minute or two later, a mist drifted across the north-east shoulder of Everest above which they were poised. As this thickened the objects gradually disappeared behind it and were lost to sight. A few minutes later the mist blew away. I looked again expecting to see them, but they had vanished as mysteriously as they had appeared.'

CHAPTER SEVEN

Traditions of another Race

The realisation that the later bloodthirsty practice of human sacrifice was founded on a corrupt memory of the days when the gods would appear on hilltops to receive the offerings placed there, must lead to a revision of the basis of many of our present assumptions. The possibility of extra-terrestrial visitors to earth is one of those factors which scholars in so many fields entirely fail to take into account. Students of mythology, for instance, have been inclined in the past to suggest that the occurrence of identical myths in different parts of the world is due to some natural process whereby the same expressions occur to all races at certain stages of cultural development. With this vague notion of the meaning of mythology, scholars have felt free to emphasise those parts which confirm their own particular theses, but have neglected to examine the true basis of the subject as a whole. In view of the striking similarity between the details and even the names which occur in the various universal myths, it is evident that they all derive from a common source. Yet no purely terrestrial theory of their origin can be found to explain the extraordinary persistence and power of their archetypal themes.

Certain incidents and anecdotes have such a compelling influence on the human mind, that it seems almost as if they reflect experiences common to everyone. The history taught in schools is more or less made up of such anecdotes, which, although attributed to historical figures, actually derive from the very earliest times of the formation of the archetypes: the story of Newton and the apple, for instance, owes its appeal to the mythical belief in the apple as the fruit by which men can acquire certain hidden knowledge. The romantic legend of Byron was strengthened by his crippled feet, through which he became associated with the gods of the underworld such as Vulcan and Wayland Smith and the Keeper of the Grail. Charlotte Corday, whose murder of Marat in his bath has so captured the popular imagination, was re-enacting the common mythical incident of the King killed in his bath by a woman. Earlier examples include the killing of Llew Llaw Gyffes, in his bath by Blodenwedd, the murder of Minos the Cretan by Cocalus and her lover Daedalus, and the murder of Agamemnon, King of Mycenæ by Clytemnestra and Aegisthus, all in similar circumstances. It is through this, its archetypal quality, that the recent legend of flying saucers, objects frequently referred to in mythology, has achieved its remarkable popularity.

The ineradicable influence of the archetypes indicates that at some time in the remote past the human race experienced an age of violent revolution, during which certain visions and themes became fixed for ever in our minds. This period is reflected in the themes of mythology. The outstanding event in the history of the world was the arrival of the force which revealed to men something of their potential. It was this which formed the archetypes that prevail today.

From a study of the earliest myths it becomes evident that the period which they record was in many ways comparable to the present time. Before the actual appearance of the gods, certain portents were observed, moving lights and mysterious discs in the sky, rumours of strange people seen unexpectedly on earth, an air of expectancy and crisis. All these things are being repeated today in a way that encourages the possibility that a repetition of the events of the past may now be imminent.

Although speculation along these lines is commonly found in science fiction and in American comics, papers so advanced and enlightened that it is sometimes hard to believe that they are not inspired, the governments of the West have done little to prepare people for the possibly imminent discovery of extra-terrestrial life. The Russian Government, it seems, has been more active. It is generally assumed that articles appearing in the press of the Soviet Union reflect official views and policy. It is all the more striking, therefore, to find in print the research and speculation of scientists such as Shklovski on the theory that extra-terrestrial life has appeared in former times on earth, maybe once, maybe on thousands of occasions. Other Soviet scientists support this theory. An article in the *Evening News* of 16 April 1962 quoted the Curator of the Palæontological Museum in Moscow, Constantin Flerov. The Museum had acquired and examined the skull of a long-horned bison found in Yakutsk in eastern Siberia. The bison had lived between 30,000 and

70,000 years ago. What had caused its death was not known, but in the centre of its forehead there was a round hole, partly healed, which Flerov and other scientists who examined the skull considered to have been made by some form of bullet. In support of their hypothesis, that the wound was made by hunters armed with projectiles, presumably from another planet, they referred to an early human skull in the British Museum, which is pierced by what appears to be two bullet holes.

An article published some years ago in the Soviet magazine *Literary Gazette* attracted a great deal of attention. In it, the two authors, Valentin Rich and Michael Chernenko discussed a theory put forward by the Russian scientist M. A. Agrest that at some time in the past the earth has been visited by people from another part of the universe. Agrest pointed out certain evidence in support of his claim.

In some parts of the world, the Libyan desert being a particular example, curious objects of a glassy substance are found called tektites. They contain radioactive isotopes, and from these it is possible roughly to date them. The process shows that they are extremely old, but not as old as the earth itself. In other words they were created some time during the world's history. Agrest suggests that they may be objects dropped long ago to earth by a space craft hovering above it in order to test the earth's atmosphere and surface.

Agrest's second suggestion is that the gigantic platform at Baalbek in the Lebanon, the largest stone of which weighs something in the region of 2,000 tons and would barely be within our power to move into position today, was constructed by visitors from space as a rocket-launching platform.

The third piece of evidence Agrest found in the Bible and other works of mythology. Stories of men coming from the sky and others, like Enoch, being lifted up to heaven refer, he says, to the times of contact between men and extra-terrestrials. Sodom and Gomorrah were destroyed by an explosion set off by an alien people from space. These men taught some of their knowledge to human beings, who retained parts of it into modern times.

The main point of Agrest's message to the Russian people was that myths and legends from the past should be re-examined without reference to their later religious and scholarly accretions and that archæologists should not dismiss conclusions that may at first seem fantastic. Not long afterwards, early in 1965 a sensational announcement on Moscow Radio quoted a report which stated that archæologists working in a cave at Ferghana in Uzbekistan had discovered prehistoric rock paintings of Martians including some showing 'a man wearing an airtight helmet with antennae and, on his back, some sort of contraption for flight'. Mr Gordon Creighton who has examined photographs of these figures says they are in fact not unlike others found in several parts of the world, and their identification with Martians is impossible to establish. But Moscow Radio's announcement was not the first claim that the caves of prehistoric artists contained representations of people from other planets.

Fig. 4 *Man and beast with the flying wheels*

A post-war expedition led by Henri Lhote explored the Tassili mountains deep in the Sahara desert, and uncovered evidence of an advanced culture which had flourished there in the remote past. Beautifully executed figures of men and animals were found painted on rock walls and preserved in good condition by the dry atmosphere. Many of the figures are highly sophisticated works of art, naturalistically executed, and show a certain Egyptian influence. Others, however, are entirely different. These are figures which Lhote considered to be the oldest of all, and seem hardly to represent human beings. They are of great size and placed on the walls in such a way that they appear to dominate all the other men and animals painted there. A striking feature of them is their heads which are round and inhuman. It seems as if they are wearing some sort of globular helmet like a diver's.

124

Because of their likeness to space men in comics and science fiction illustrations, Lhote and his party called these creatures 'Martians'. Lhote later denied that there was any significance in this name or that he seriously thought that the figures were really those of extra-terrestrials. Nevertheless the idea persisted. The pictures of 'Martians' in the Sahara desert became widely known; newspapers and magazine articles revealed the popularity of the belief that they might be portraits of past visitors from space. Shklovski, the Soviet scientist, took the idea seriously, and used it to illustrate his belief that an alien civilisation has at some time in the remote past appeared on earth. It may be that Lhote was entirely frivolous when he called the painted giants 'Martians', but for all that there is considerable significance in the fact that he did so. The tradition of extra-terrestrials and how they are supposed to look is one that has not changed in thousands of years. The peculiar little bronze figures of men found in Sardinia, one of which has four eyes and a cap with two knobbed antennae protruding, are good examples of the antiquity of the popular conception of space men. When Lhote saw the Sahara giants he thought of Martians as shown in comics, etc. But this popular idea of how Martians look is based on a long tradition in which fairies, monsters, ghosts, supernatural creatures of all sorts play a part. To these can be added the 'little green men' associated with flying saucers, helmeted astronauts and other similar figures from modern history and imagination, all of which derive from the same archetype. Our idea of what an extra-terrestrial should look like is a mixture of all these figures, a legacy of actual experience in the remote past, reinforced ever since by occasional rumours of their reappearance. It might, therefore, be that the Frenchmen's impulse to call the giant, helmeted figures of the Sahara 'Martians' was of deeper significance than they themselves realised.

The Sahara giants are not the only figures of antiquity to have been claimed as representation of former visitors from space. Deep in the forests of southern Vera Cruz in Mexico enormous stones are found carved into the shape of heads, each wearing what seems to be a tight-fitting helmet. Some see them as the gods of the Olmecs, a mysterious race long extinct, but no tradition has survived to explain their meaning. The same is true of certain other early Mexican figurines, remarkably like the modern figure of a helmeted space man.

A peculiar feature of the early American civilisations is that they do not appear to have originated on that continent. The semi-legendary race of architects and craftsmen, by whom the civilised arts were traditionally first introduced, arrived in Central America with a fully developed culture, which subsequently appears to have declined. The leader of the Toltecs, the plumed serpent Quetzalcoatl, is said to have been a white man with fair hair and a beard dressed in robes, who came from the sky with his band of followers bringing the gifts of civilisation to the American continent. Thor Heyerdahl and others believe that images of these people survive in the giant stone figures found in South America, particularly in the region of Lake Titicaca, and in the extraordinary statues of Easter Island, which appear to represent men with European features and red hair, for they wear on their heads red stone caps, quarried from a different area to the stone from which the figures themselves are made.

The sudden arrival in Central America of these people with their evolved culture has encouraged those who believe in the former existence of a great continent, Atlantis, now lost beneath the ocean. The theory of Atlantis and of Mu, the lost continent which Churchward placed in the central Pacific, is extremely old and persistent. This semi-legendary land is mentioned by classical authors and appears in Celtic legend as the Fortunate Isles, a country lying far away to the West, where men never age, food and drink are abundant, and everything is perfect. To this land are ferried the souls of the dead and above it hovers the glass tower, the stronghold of the gods. Later accounts of Atlantis, such as those of Bacon and Donnelly, describe it as the centre of a great civilisation, a land of tall buildings and fine cities, whose inhabitants preserved the knowledge inherited from the gods together with the art of flying and of communicating with each other over long distances. In fact, although many theories of the terrestrial location of Atlantis have been put forward, it was evidently not a country of this world. There may indeed have been a mid-Atlantic island now engulfed by the sea, but, if so, it contributed little to the Atlantis legend. It was not from some lost continent that civilisation reached America and elsewhere, but from somewhere outside the earth, the land from which Quetzalcoatl, travelling on the serpent raft or flying disc, brought the vision of the gods to men.

If the stone heads of America and the red-headed giants of Easter Island are seen as representing a fair race of civilising gods, a faint but authentic memory of these same people survives also across the

126

Pacific in Australia. Of all the places where the primitive art of rock painting has flourished, only among the Australian Aborigines is it still practised, and they are now the only people to retain an oral tradition of its meaning. For the most part there is little remarkable in Australian rock painting. Animals and birds more or less naturalistically drawn, together with outlines of human and animal footmarks, stylised weapons and objects of everyday use are found all over the continent, and are not unlike those from other parts of the world. One figure, however, appears only in Australia and then in only one corner of the continent, the Kimberley Mountain area of Western Australia. Here are found the most extraordinary paintings, which, since their first discovery in 1838 have aroused a great deal of curiosity. These are the figures called by the natives Wondjina.

The Wondjina are anthropomorphic figures, considered by the Aborigines to be extremely sacred. They are painted either singly or in rows on exposed rocks or in rock shelters, upright and staring outwards from the walls. Their faces and shoulders are white and contain only three features, the eyes and nose, each shown large and black, the effect being of a man wearing a sort of white gas mask. They never have mouths, and it appears from the natives that the lack of this feature is in some way essential to the Wondjina's character. Round their heads like an inverted horseshoe they wear a red band, as it might be a helmet or stylised wig. Sometimes another horseshoe is shown outside the first. Where their bodies are included in the portrait, they are clothed in long striped robes.

The first Wondjina to be seen by a European were found by George Grey in 1838 in a remote region near Glenelg River, Western Australia, at a spot apparently never since revisited. The figures he drew, though unmistakably of the same type as those later found elsewhere, differ from them in several ways. Above all, the red band round the head is, as Grey drew it, obviously a halo, and on the halo appear certain marks which look like characters in writing. The striking thing about these characters is that they also appear carved on stones in certain parts of South America. Professor Homet, who examined these carved stones, concluded that the marks were made at least 10,000 and as long as 30,000 years ago. What is more, Homet remarked that they were exactly the same as the hieroglyphics in the message which George Adamski received after his meeting in 1952 with a being he described as a Venusian in the Californian desert.

127

Professor Homet, while having no particular interest in flying saucers, is one of those scientists who now believe that a great civilisation existed on earth before ours, with a knowledge of flight and of atomic power. He draws no conclusion from the similarity between the hieroglyphs in Adamski's book, which was published before his own, and the rock marks reproduced in his book *Sons of the Sun*. But the fact that these marks are the same as those which Grey found on the halo round the head of the Aborigines' sacred figure, the Wondjina, must strengthen the belief that the Wondjina paintings are portraits of a superior people once known in other parts of the world and everywhere identified with the immortal gods.

Grey's discovery aroused considerable interest at the time, and attempts were made to explain the figures as relics of a religious cult, perhaps introduced by early missionaries. At all events it was admitted that Grey's Wondjina provided evidence that European colonists may not have been the first civilised visitors to Australia. This view is supported by the Aborigines themselves. The Wondjina, they say, are people who came to Australia in the earliest times, and, in a way, are still alive. At their first appearance they came as creators, forming the landscape and establishing all the institutions of native life. When their work was done, they entered a cave and died, a companion painting their portraits on the rock wall. They then passed on to another plane of existence. They are still responsible for the continuation of natural life, the birth of babies, the coming of rain, all aspects of fertility, and, to maintain their power, the natives retouch their portraits at a certain time of the year, a duty which they strictly observe.

Upon one thing the Aborigines are insistent. Although they admit to their race having painted all the other rock figures, they absolutely deny having had anything to do with the portraits of the Wondjina. The creatures whom the portraits represent did them themselves when they were on earth. Now they have returned to the sky, and can be seen at night as lights moving high above the earth, but since their creative work was completed they have not openly reappeared.

The discovery that the Australian natives are aware of strange moving lights in the sky is interesting as such phenomena are frequently reported by white Australians today. No other country has produced more flying saucer reports or shown such interest in the subject, and it appears that even the early explorers saw things which are hard to explain. On the tragic expedition across the continent which Burke and Wills undertook in 1860, the only survivor, King, had a vision, recorded by Wills in his diary.

'Near daybreak, King reported seeing a moon in the east, with a haze of light stretching up from it; he declared it to be quite as large as the moon, and not dim at the edges.'

The Aborigines do not see time as a fixed and orderly force, moving ever onwards at the same pace, but as a kind of lake where movement in any direction can be made. The Wondjina, which to Europeans are unreal figures, living only in myth, are to them just as material as are the kangaroos, snakes and other animals painted alongside them. They are associated with the lights in the sky, such as that seen by King. The Aborigines believe these lights to be the embodiment of their ancestors, the creators of their world; thus the Wondjina and the strange lights are identical. A feature of native art, which has a considerable bearing on the meaning of the Wondjina, is that Aborigines are above all naturalistic painters. Apart from a few conventional stylisations and decorative motifs, all the figures they paint on rock surfaces are taken from life, often accurately detailed. Among the more modern pictures found in the Kimberley area some show Japanese sailors and soldiers in nineteenth-century uniform; there is an early Dutch colonist in clogs, and a remarkable Crucifixion scene, with natives nailed to the cross and centurions in the uniform of the Royal Australian Air Force. It would be strange if the Wondjina were the only purely imaginary figures in the Aborigines' rock galleries, and it is presumptuous of Europeans to dismiss them as such, simply because the creatures they represent have not appeared during the short period of European colonisation. The natives have an explanation for all their pictures, including those of the first colonists, and when they say that the Wondjina were early visitors to Australia it is hard to disbelieve them on that point alone; particularly since similar beings, men with white skin and fair hair play such an important part in the early legends of Central and South America.

Besides the legends which explain the Wondjina portraits, there are other indications that the Aborigines were once in contact with a superior race of creative, civilising people. It is clear that at one time they formed a far more advanced and organised society than they do now, and left to themselves would eventually have degenerated to the level of the Tasmanians, exterminated in 1878, who had lost almost every vestige of culture, including any form of coherent religion.

Certain of the Aborigines' artefacts are outstanding. The boomerang, for example, is something far above their present level of culture. In a stagnant society like that of the Aborigines, the evolution of such a sophisticated object would be inconceivable. There can be no doubt that it is a survival from times when the laws of aerodynamics on which it is based were actively studied. The fact that some tribes have entirely forgotten the use of it, and others keep it only as a toy shows how easily it might have been lost in the general decline of Aboriginal culture.

Other evidence for the existence of a former civilisation can be seen in the frequently quoted instances of scientific knowledge embedded in tribal custom and taboos; the extraordinary rules of hygiene, genetics and game preservation which primitive people obey without any conscious knowledge of the principles behind them. Yet the strictness with which these rules are enforced within the tribe, and the interest which its members show in their observance (Lévi-Strauss says that he has met members of primitive tribes who have a deep interest in anthropology particularly among the Australian Aborigines, some of whom send observers to study the customs of other tribes, apparently in order to maintain the correctness of their own) indicates an awareness of their intrinsic merit. No human lawgiver is ever reputed to have framed these codes; they are always the legacy of a superior race. Hebrew mythology tells of Moses receiving a code of laws from God himself on a mountain top, and other races have legends of this sort to illustrate the institution of law and order, and the creation of a rigid code of behaviour. Often, it is said, the laws were first imposed by a force from the sky, sometimes by the serpent as the sky-gods' representative, sometimes by a vanished race of wise men who introduced the arts of civilisation. The story of Hine-rangi and her heavenly lover, quoted in a previous chapter, is a Maori version of how contact with an enlightened people from outside the earth led to the birth of human civilisation.

It is impossible to explain the persistence among primitive societies of the elaborate systems of rules necessary for their survival without concluding that they must at one time in the remote past have been

130

deliberately drawn up by people fully aware of their significance, and also conscious of the necessity for established rituals to ensure their continued observance. It seems that the first steps in civilisation were not taken spontaneously by the human race alone – the point has been made that after man had existed in a state of nature for hundreds of thousands of years without showing the least inclination to make even the first move towards developing a culture it seems impossible that it could have been an internal stimulus which led to the first move being made – but came about as the result of contact with an external race. The human beings who were close to or were directly instructed by the gods, together with their descendants, the heroes of mythology, introduced what they themselves had learnt to the rest of humanity, which at that time was few in number and confined to small areas of the earth's surface. They themselves, those who had had direct, first-hand knowledge of the gods and their ways, formed a kind of élite, devoting themselves to preserving the scholarship they had acquired, which the mass of people were yet unable to appreciate.

This was the origin of what Theosophists call the Arcane Tradition, the mysterious hidden store of knowledge which has survived from the very earliest times until the present day.

The whole subject of what Hallam called 'the hidden stream of esoteric truth' is to the highest degree controversial, and has been at times, perhaps purposely, obscured by extravagant and fantastic claims. But it does seem that in many parts of the world, alongside the open, fashionable beliefs and customs of the day, there has been a deeper, unchanging tradition preserved from times of the remotest antiquity. This tradition, kept alive often by an élite caste within a minority or subject race, has provided a link between one age and civilisation and another, occasionally emerging to some extent into the open to refresh and stimulate the prevailing philosophy of the times. So that the spirit and content of this tradition may be comprehensible to men of all cultures, ages and nations, it is expressed through the medium of allegoric poetry, the one form of language common to the entire human race. Robert Graves in *The White Goddess* describes the Welsh minstrels of the Middle Ages of a non-Cymric race, 'a mixture of Goidels, Brythons, Bronze Age and New Stone Age peoples and Aboriginals'. They 'went from village to village, or farm-house to farm-house, entertaining under the trees or in the chimney corner according to the season. It was they who kept alive an astonishingly ancient literary tradition, mainly in the form of popular tales which preserved fragments not only of pre-Cymric, but of pre-Goidelic myth some of which goes back as far as the Stone Age.'

The poems and tales of the wandering British minstrels were indeed of almost unimaginable antiquity; they finally passed into the native folklore so avidly collected by nineteenth-century scholars. But they were simply degenerate survivals of a complete and highly sophisticated system of history, philosophy and science which had flourished in Britain up to the beginning of historical times, and whose later keepers were the Druids.

It has lately been fashionable, in reaction against eighteenth-century enthusiasm, to denigrate the Druids as a learned body. It is true that they were hardly concerned with the evolution of original philosophy or with any advancement of culture. They regarded themselves simply as custodians and codifiers of a system of knowledge inherited from those who came before them. Yet their reputation as learned and honourable men was famous all over Europe. The Romans recognised their advanced religious and astronomical knowledge. Julius Caesar said of them, 'Many young men assemble in their colleges of their own accord or are sent by parents and relations. It is said that they learn there a great number of verses by heart. Some therefore stay for twenty years under instruction. . . . They have discussions about the stars and their movements, the size of the universe and of the earth, the order of nature and the strength and powers of the immortal gods. Their knowledge they hand down to the young men.'

And according to Pomponius Mela, 'They profess to know the size and shape of the world, the movements of the heavens and of the stars and the will of the gods'.

Rich men from all over northern Europe sent their sons to study with the Druids in Britain. Even after their suppression by the Romans it is recorded that the son of a King of Scotland was sent to a surviving Druid college in the Isle of Man. As in the religious colleges of India, their learning was expressed in a series of verses. This does not imply simply the composition of rhymes and riddles which could easily be learned by heart, but the use of a poetic language, a way of expressing ideas so that their true meaning was hidden from anyone who did not have the poetic key. Through this medium, the poetic lingua franca, which transcends all barriers of language, race and time, the Druids had received their knowledge of the nature of God, the true history and origin of the human race and the shape of the universe from their predecessors, the creators of amazing astronomical instruments such as Stonehenge. These Stone Age people had in turn received their traditions from an earlier age reaching back to the remotest days when the archetypes were formed, the times of open knowledge of the gods themselves.

A certain amount of poetic lore survived the collapse of organised Druidism and became the stock-in-trade of the professional minstrels and story-tellers who flourished in the Middle Ages. In many cases it degenerated into doggerel so meaningless that even with a complete knowledge of the images it originally contained nothing can be made of it today. But as vestiges of Druidic worship it could be noted in Wales and other remote areas in comparatively recent times (a huge image of Hu Gadarn the serpent god was only discovered in Wales in the reign of Henry VIII and taken to Smithfield in London to be burnt together with the priest who served it), some of the knowledge which the Druids had preserved survived in oral tradition long after Druidism had perished. The most extraordinary example, revealed in a dramatic way, was the popular awareness of the two satellites of Mars long before modern astronomers suspected their existence.

Dean Swift drew on this tradition for his book *Gulliver's Travels*, written in 1727. He described how the astronomers of the flying island of Laputa had discovered 'two lesser stars, or satellites, which revolve about Mars, whereof the innermost is distant from the centre of the primary planet exactly three of his diameters, the outermost five; the former revolves in the space of ten hours, the latter in twenty-one and a half'. Voltaire repeated the same story in *Micromégas* written in 1750.

In 1877, a century and a half after *Gulliver's Travels*, Asaph Hall, the American astronomer, became the first man to see the Mars satellites through a telescope. What he discovered confirmed in an amazing way their description by Swift. The two satellites, named by Hall Phobos and Deimos, are placed and behave so much according to how Swift described them that the possibility of a chance coincidence can hardly be considered. What is more both Phobos and Deimos are very peculiar bodies indeed. Phobos is only about 3,700 miles from the surface of Mars and is unique in appearing to rise in the west and set in the east. Its course across the sky takes only $4\frac{1}{4}$ hours. Deimos, on the other hand, is visible from any one spot on Mars for sixty hours at a time. The famous Russian astrophysicist, Shklovski, who has made a study of the two satellites has concluded from calculations of its orbit in relation to its mass that Phobos must be hollow, and is in all probability an artificial satellite launched many years ago from the surface of Mars. The same would apply to Deimos. If this is true, there can only be one answer to the question of how their existence was known from early times on earth. There must have been a tradition preserved from some time in the past when an extra-terrestrial race introduced their knowledge of the universe, knowledge gained by ages of study and by actual experience of travel among the other planets. The mystery of the extraordinary astronomical lore possessed by some primitive races can be explained in these terms; so can that of more advanced people who inherited complicated systems of measuring time based on astronomic observations, yet lacked the instruments which these systems imply. The Mayan calendar, around which the whole life of those people revolved must certainly have been the result of hundreds of years' observation, for the cycles of the sun, the moon, the planet Venus and other bodies on which it is based extend over great periods of time. Yet there is no sign of this calendar having evolved. It seems to have been an integral part of Mayan culture, something which at a certain moment in history emerged fully formed from some hidden stream of knowledge.

If we accept that a genuine tradition of vast antiquity did in fact survive into historical times, the whole of our attitude towards early 'mythical' history will have to be revised. Scholars have analysed the various universal myths from every point of view except that which allows for their true reflection of historical events at the dawn of human civilisation. The possibility of a true oral tradition surviving the vast period between, say, the introduction of fire and the invention of writing has never been taken seriously enough for it to have formed the basis for a scientific revaluation of mythology. Yet only by accepting this assumption can mythology be given any true and organic meaning.

CHAPTER EIGHT

The Dragon, the Holy Grail, and the Flying Saucer

Ophiolatry, the worship of the sacred serpent is an expression of the flying saucer cult which is the basis of all religion. In Britain the serpent cult flourished among the Druids, even in Ireland and the Isle of Man where snakes cannot live, an indication that the serpent was merely the symbol of the true object of veneration, the flying disc for which, as we have seen, it so often stands. We know that the early Britons looked to the sky for their gods; their adoption of the serpent as the object of their cult reveals their desire to attract and propitiate the heavenly dragon, the shining, spinning disc.

The worship of the serpent and the winged disc as the fundamental British cult was first discovered in the seventeenth century by Dr Stukely, a scholar of such perception that he may even have realised something of the implications of his theory, for in his later work, since derided and now little known, he concluded that the great prehistoric monuments of Wessex and other parts of England were constructed in such a way that they formed a great pattern, comprehensible only when viewed from the air. With this he must have come close to identifying the sacred serpent or winged disc with the airships of a former divine race. Since Stukely's time, so much evidence has been found to support his theories, that an impartial reassessment of his whole work is overdue. His only recent biographer, Professor Piggott, merely describes him in the narrow terms of modern archæology, the students of which, unlike Stukely but like those of most sciences and professions today, seem to be trained to ask questions of interest only to their own circles with no bearing on the larger problems with which they should be concerned.

Many of the greatest monuments of antiquity were laid out for three reasons; first, as instruments for the study of the nature of the gods and the patterns of the universe; secondly, as meeting places with people of the divine race, often on sites where, in the past, the

135

gods had been known to appear, and thirdly, to give by their shape and outline some message, visible and comprehensible only to the gods in the sky.

In Stonehenge these three aims were achieved. The American astronomer, Hawkins, has proved mathematically that the stones of the monument form an incredibly accurate observatory and computer, which records the phases of the sun and the cycle of eclipses, a conclusion which was earlier reached by Sir Norman Lockyer. Just as early Christian churches were placed on sites of pre-Christian sanctity, a building such as Stonehenge would have been placed at a spot already considered holy, perhaps as a place where the gods had once revealed themselves to men. In the same way the chapels at Lourdes and Fatima were built at the places where the heavenly lady came down to earth. A reference to the gods appearing at Stonehenge comes in the work of a sixth-century historian, Hecateus, quoted by Diodorus Siculus.

'On this island (Britain) is a magnificent grove of Apollo and a remarkable temple, circular in shape, adorned with many consecrated gifts. . . . It is said that in this island the moon appears very near to the earth, that certain eminences of a terrestrial form are plainly seen on it, that Apollo visits the island once in the course of nineteen years, in which period the stars complete their revolutions and that for this reason the Greeks distinguish the cycle of nineteen years by the name of "the great year". During this season of his appearance the god plays upon the harp and dances every night from the vernal equinox until the rising of the Pleiads, pleased with his own successes.'

The remarkable thing about Stonehenge is the way in which its form exactly reflects the conventional image of the flying saucer. The similarity is unmistakable when the monument is viewed from above. There is the well defined outer rim consisting of a low bank and ditch. Inside this are the Aubrey holes, small circular pits set in a ring around the perimeter just like the portholes so often reported in flying saucers and also found in ancient representations of the flying saucer from Asia, Greece and Crete. In the centre is the perfect stone circle of the raised cabin, enclosing the horseshoe-shaped trilithon construction which appears above the surrounding rim like a dome or

136

cockpit. The smaller bluestones stand inside the circle and are visible through its openings as were the men in the mysterious flying object which in 1959 hovered over a mission school in New Guinea in full view of the teachers and pupils. It seems likely that these stones which were brought from Wales were originally set up elsewhere to mark places of contact between men and gods and that they were taken to Stonehenge to represent the gods themselves inside their vehicle.

As a reproduction of the flying saucer, Stonehenge is evidently a sort of cargo cult monument, a pattern of the sacred disc, built to attract this object for which men felt such a yearning. The belief that it was planned to be seen from above is shared by Dr Gerhard Wiebe, Dean of the Boston School of Public Communications, who said, quoted by Hawkins,

'Stonehenge makes no sense when seen from the ground. It is impressive only when seen in plan from above. But neolithic man had no aeroplanes from which to view his own work – therefore he may have been signalling his powers to the gods in the sky . . . to his gods.'

If Stonehenge was intended to reproduce the form of the flying disc, it is evidently one of those circular temples which the Mexicans say were only built after the coming of the sky god, Quetzalcoatl. In fact W. S. Blackett in *The Lost Histories of America* compares Stonehenge with certain ancient American structures, and concludes that they may have had an identical origin. His theory that it was built by early travellers from America sounds fantastic although there is evidence that in prehistoric times the Atlantic was less of a barrier than it later became. Some Indian tribes believe that it was they who discovered Europe rather than vice versa, and as late as 1508 a boat full of American Indians was sighted by a French vessel not far off the coast of England. But whoever it was that built Stonehenge, a monument unique in northern Europe, its striking similarity to the flying saucer and its association with the sky god indicate that it was a cult object in the worship of the heavenly disc.

This aspect of the meaning of Stonehenge is supported by the appearance of another type of structure lying near Stonehenge and connected to it by an avenue. This is the mysterious enclosure known as the Cursus, whose low earth banks stretch in two parallel lines, never more than a hundred yards apart, for nearly two miles, curving in a semi-circle to meet each other at the two ends. Other than as a sign to be seen from the sky, the Cursus has no obvious practical use, but its shape, that of an elongated cigar, is the same as that of the other type of UFO commonly seen, the long, shadowy object often described as a sort of aircraft carrier from which the smaller discs are launched. It may well be that the Cursus is a reproduction of such a craft, for a large number of disc barrows cluster round it, and, at the western end actually appear as though emerging from inside its banks.

The practice of laying out huge symbols on the ground in such a way, that they only had any significance when viewed from above, was at one time not uncommon. In certain parts of the world figures of men, animals and fish have been found carved on the horizontal faces of rocks, a form of art which was only recently abandoned by the natives of Australia. Some of these figures are very large, but nowhere else are they on anything like the scale of the amazing lines etched into the Nazca plains of Peru. It was not until a few years ago, when the first aeroplanes flew over this area that they were discovered, for they are so large that from ground level they are quite invisible. Two Peruvian pilots who were the first men to fly over the plains were astonished to see below them great figures, shapes and circles and straight lines stretching out for many miles along the ground. Among them were the outlines of figures, including whales, birds and spiders, and what appears to be a man wearing a helmet. The German scientist, Dr Maria Reiche, who has studied these extraordinary figures, concludes that they are extremely old, certainly from a time before the civilisation of the Incas, and were made by a mysterious race, all memory and trace of which the Incas seem deliberately to have blotted out. The lines have been made by removing a layer of stones from the surface of the desert soil in an area so dry that after, maybe, thousands of years they do not appear to have deteriorated. It is impossible that men without aeroplanes could ever have seen them, for even from an elevation of a few hundred feet they are invisible. Probably the Incas themselves never knew the secret. They constructed a road right through the centre of the lines as if ignorant of their existence. Naturally modern writers have linked the Nazca lines with the subject of flying saucers, and some have speculated whether they may indicate certain natural lines of force of the sort along which flying saucers are sometimes said to move. This theory was strengthened by the rediscovery of two remarkable books written in the 1920s by A. Watkins of Hereford.

The first of these books, *Early British Trackways*, later amplified into *The Old Straight Track* described how Mr Watkins, in the course of visiting ancient sites in Herefordshire remarked that many of these sites could be joined together by drawing a straight line on the map. He then found that these lines could be protracted to pass through other places of interest. These included churches built on prehistoric sites, hill-tops, old dew ponds, moats and single trees, often those with a name or local reputation. The lines also took in stone circles, standing stones and earthworks. Mr Watkins' later book described his further work on the subject. Straight lines, which he called leys, are to be found all over England, some stretching for a considerable distance and linking many of the sites of antiquity in the area. Only by walking along these leys can their validity be confirmed. Later disciples of Mr Watkins, organised into a club by Mr J. Goddard, have done some remarkable field work, filling out existing leys with crossroads, farms with names peculiar to those situated on leys, and uncharted stones and other monuments of the past. Whereas Watkins supposed that the leys were ancient footpaths, modern ley explorers are inclined to see them as having some meaning as lines only to be seen from above. Watkins' theory is made absurd by the fact that many of the leys pass through bogs, over precipices and into places which no track could penetrate, an objection to which he gave the extraordinary answer that travellers in the past may have had a different way of thinking. And he encouraged later theorists by quoting a case where a friend of his, who possessed a hilltop grove of trees, situated directly on a ley, was asked by the Air Ministry not to cut them down as they provided a useful landmark for pilots. Indeed it does seem more likely that leys had, like the Nazca lines, some significance only from the sky. Attempts to align them with the chart of modern flying saucer observations have so far been inconclusive. But what is remarkable is that the old sites of sacrifice to the sky-gods, hilltops and artificial mounds are regularly linked by systems of leys. Several pass through the great artificial pyramid of England, the sacrificial Silbury Hill. Here the Roman road follows the course of a ley. Others intersect at Cley Hill, one of the meeting places between men and gods, which stands above Warminster and has recently been the centre of a great wave of flying saucer observations. The discovery that the high places were once linked together by lines and landmarks significant only from the air substantiates the legend that these places were the centre of a sky-god cult, raised platforms where contact with the flying gods was made and sacrifices offered.

It now appears that there is evidence for the existence of leys in other parts of the world and of their connection with the routes taken by flying saucers.

In his curious little book, *The Chinese Dragon*, L. N. Hayes says that the Chinese recognise certain straight lines stretching over the globe corresponding to the lines along which fiery dragons fly between their hilltop homes. The land over which these lines run was considered particularly fortunate and no one could be buried or build a house there without the Emperor's consent. The founder of the Sung dynasty, Chao Ming, having to move his father's bones from their old burial place, chanced to choose a spot on one of the Lung Mei or dragon paths for their reinterment. Ever afterwards he prospered, and from being a poor, obscure man he finally became Emperor. Hayes tells another story of an incident which happened not many years ago. A Chinese student, returning from Japan, committed suicide on the ship. His friends buried him in a valley through which ran a Lung Mei. When the authorities came to know of this, they sent urgent telegrams to the local magistrates demanding the student's disinterment and the Board of Rites in Peking became anxious about the matter. The student's body was moved, but it is said that after the Revolution, it was replaced in the original grave.

At least until recently the overwhelming majority of Chinese believed in the physical existence of dragons. Since they appear to be identical with the Western concept of flying saucers – they are often reported as moving lights in the sky and their appearance is taken as a portent of events to come – the discovery that dragons move over the earth's surface on certain straight lines will encourage those who are working to compare leys with the routes of flying saucers.*

Our recently renewed awareness of the mysterious objects in the sky makes it increasingly urgent for us to discover how these objects were interpreted in the past. Clues from early religious beliefs,

* Lung Mei, straight lines linking the places associated with the dragon, have been traced in Britain.

mythology and folklore indicate that flying saucers were seen as the vehicles of a divine race and that they were associated with many of the sites where they are said to appear today. The old cult of the winged serpent, which Stukely deduced, and the dragon legend provide a direct link between modern flying saucer reports and those of the past. All over England there are hills, natural or artificial associated with the appearance of a fiery dragon or giant worm. The worm, the Anglo-Saxon word for the Chinese dragon, emerges from a well or pit like the fire-bearing serpent of the Ainu legend. It coils itself round a circular hill and from there devastates the country, demanding various kinds of tribute until despatched by a local hero. The most famous of these hills is Dragon Hill, an artificial looking mound just below the great chalk figure of the White Horse cut in the Berkshire downs.

The whole area around the White Horse was one of the great centres of the sky-god cult. The Horse itself, placed near the summit of the hill in such a way that it is visible in its entirety only from the air, is the best known of several similar monuments unique to England, whose dates can never be accurately estimated but which are certainly hundreds, maybe thousands of years old. Of the few other hill figures which survive or whose past existence is suspected the two most remarkable are the Cerne Abbas giant and the Long Man at Wilmington. The giant wields a club and displays a huge phallus, a feature which he retained in spite of the sensitivity of the nineteenth century because of local objections to his mutilation. The Long Man, disarmed and emasculated by early Christians, is now left only with two poles which he holds in outstretched hands. Both these figures, like the White Horse, were made as landmarks to be seen from the sky, and indicated a sacred sacrificial spot on the summits of the hills on which they stand. Above the White Horse lies the circular earthwork, Uffington Castle, the scene of the feasts and games which Thomas Hughes describes in *The Scouring of the White Horse*. But the true sacred spot is Dragon Hill, the circular mound just below, whose round flat summit is like that of Silbury and of those other mounds associated with the dragon legend. It was here that the dragon was killed by St George, or, as was said locally, King George, a reminder that the Christian saint is a later substitution for some local hero. A bare patch on the top of Dragon Hill where no grass grows is said to have been caused by the poisonous blood of the

141

dragon in his death throes. Other sacred hilltop sites in Britain are similarly marked by a spot of bare earth, a famous example being the grassless plot on the hilltop mound where Montgomery church now stands. In this case a later legend, that of a thief wrongly executed on whose grave no grass will grow, has taken over from the original tradition of a bare patch on the hilltop caused by the landing of a winged disc. The haunted reputation of Dragon Hill led Dr Rose, a past curate of the neighbouring village of Baulking, to write the following verse, sometimes attributed to a local squire, the dimmest of all Poet Laureates, Pym.

> '*Where oft it has reported been*
> *That spectres have at dusk been seen,*
> *And fleeting ghosts and visions dire,*
> *And serpents green, and flames of fire,*
> *And hideous sounds, as we are told,*
> *That cow the spirits of the bold,*
>   *But can not be expressed.*'

Dragon Hill is so similar in shape and general appearance to the other English mounds associated with the flying saucer legend that to see it for the first time is to experience an immediate sense of recognition. As with all such former places of sacrifice there must somewhere nearby be the site of a pre-Christian temple. This can be found by following the road from Dragon Hill to the village of Uffington in the plain below, where the church now occupies what is obviously a site of ancient religious significance, a slightly raised circular mound. It was from here that the sacrifices to the sky-gods were taken to be exposed on Dragon Hill.

Two miles along the Ridgeway from the White Horse stands a monument whose legendary association with a flying god, unique in Britain, confirms the significance of the whole area as a former centre of the sky-god cult. The monument, a ruined dolmen known as Wayland Smith's cave, was said to be the haunt of the blacksmith of the gods, Wieland, a figure of German and Scandinavian mythology. In his youth Wieland, together with his brother Eigil, the original hero of the William Tell legend, had had an adventure with women of an alien race, the legendary 'swan maidens', and it may have been from them that he acquired a knowledge of the art of flight. A king, hearing of his skill as a blacksmith, crippled him and confined him to an island where he was put to work. Like the Chinese emperor, Shun, and like Daedalus on his flight from Crete, Wieland made a contrivance for flight and escaped from his prison by air. It is appropriate that Wieland, a man who inherited something of the gods' skill at flying, should be associated with the area of the White Horse, the sign to the gods in the sky.

On any journey through England it is possible to detect various hills and high places where once the gods came down to receive their sacrifices. The discovery and recognition of these places is an exciting occupation, which experience makes even more rewarding. They can be identified in a number of ways. There are those hills, already mentioned, which stand above and are connected with a stone circle or a site of pre-Christian worship. Since the message of Pope Gregory in 601, advising Christians to place their churches on the sites of earlier temples, a great many churches now mark the place once occupied by a stone circle or sacred mound. As Alcroft points

Fig. 5 The Lycian symbol of the figure in the spinning disc

out in his book *The Cross and the Circle*, these sites can often be recognised where a church stands in a circular graveyard particularly where, as is often the case, the churchyard appears to be artificially raised above the surrounding land. It often happens that the circular form of a graveyard has been preserved by a road making a curve round part of its circumference while the rest of the circle has been destroyed and the boundaries of the graveyard rearranged in rectangular form. But sometimes in the remoter parts of the country, particularly Wales, the entire original shape of the graveyard has been preserved, and the church can be seen to stand on a raised circular mound. For a considerable time after the introduction of Christianity the circle retained its significance as the symbol of the gods, the link between heaven and earth, and to be buried within the sign of the circle was a respected custom. On the outside of many churches, in the flintwork of the tower or porch, the circle can also be seen as well as the spiral and the three-legged device within the wheel, representing like the Celtic cross the continuation of the old symbol long after it had officially been replaced by the new. Wherever a church placed within the pre-Christian circle stands in a significant relationship with a dramatically shaped hill, the existence of a former place of sacrifice can be suspected.

Other hills, once the meeting places between the gods and men, include those situated on leys, those whose summits are surrounded by earthworks built to protect and enclose the holy spot, those where midsummer fires and beacons were lit and those with a local reputation for being the haunt of fairies and supernatural beings. A further example of the continuing association between certain hilltops and the gods from space can be seen in the number of hills and headlands dedicated to St George or St Michael. These two figures appear to be Christian versions of Castor and Pollux, the heavenly twins, whose home was in a distant star. St Michael is a most interesting figure. He is the leader of the host of angels who received Enoch on his journey to heaven and told him of the 'word' by which the universe was created. It is he who Daniel says will appear at that time of chaos preceding the Millennium. In Christian hagiology Michael seems to be the descendant of some former revered being, associated with high places and with the killing of a dragon. The number of churches dedicated to St Michael which stand on hilltops and pre-Christian mounds is remarkable. Evidently all their sites were once associated with the memory of a being from the sky and of the dragon disc. In the West Country particularly, a great number of churches set on high mounds are dedicated to St Michael. Of these much the most famous is the ruined tower of Glastonbury Tor.

It is hardly surprising that the Glastonbury area, one of the most strikingly beautiful in the country, has always been a great religious centre. The steep, conical hill with its flat top towers over the surrounding plain as once it rose from the flooded countryside, forming the sort of island mountain most strongly associated with the legend of the sky gods. Here is Avalon, the paradise of Arthurian romance.

144

From Glastonbury Tor men left earth to join the gods. Its reputation as a place of sacrifice must have been alive in the sixteenth century, for in 1539 a ritual was performed there which echoed events in the remote past.

The wealth of Glastonbury Abbey had attracted the attention of Henry VIII and his agent Thomas Cromwell. An excuse was found to remove the abbot, Richard Whiting who, together with two other monks was condemned to death. The three victims were dragged on hurdles up the steep sides of the Tor. There on the flat summit they were hanged. So Glastonbury Tor became another of the sacred high places where the erection of a gibbet perverted the old practice of offering men to the gods from the sky.

Glastonbury Tor is so obviously a sacrificial hill that one would expect to find there one of the dragon legends with which these places are so often associated. All the usual features are present; it is conical with a flat top, and scored around with deep grooves such as are frequently said on other hills to have been caused by the coils of a serpent encircling it; not far away is the usual sacred well or pool, in this case the Chalice Well, from which the Serpent emerges; above all it is related to a nearby site of great sanctity, now occupied by the ruins of Glastonbury Abbey. Here grows the famous Glastonbury thorn, said to have sprung from the staff of St Joseph of Arimathea and to flower every Christmas Day, which in fact forms the last remains of a pre-Christian grove. Holy thorns such as this – Hudson recorded another on Salisbury Plain where as late as the nineteenth century a condemned murderer stopped to pray on the way to his execution – and single trees of particular sanctity are closely linked with stone circles and standing stones. Trees or bushes mark the spot where gods have appeared to men. The fiery vision which Moses saw in the desert, the angels of Joan of Arc and the Lady of Fatima all appeared by a low tree. Even Howard Menger was given a spot beside a tree for a meeting place with his space girls. When in due course the tree where the vision took place decayed, it was replaced by a stone pillar, to mark the spot where the tree had stood. The special sanctity of the spot as a place where a god had appeared on earth became transferred to the stone. Later, stones were removed from their original sites and re-erected in circles, like the Welsh blue stones of Stonehenge, perhaps following the conquest of the territory where they stood by another tribe. The practice of replacing a holy tree with a stone pillar was observed even into the nineteenth century when an oak at Hoxne in Suffolk, associated with the martyrdom of St Edmund, blew down and a stone was erected in its place; and there are certainly even later examples. Stone pillars were also set up to mark the spot where an encounter with an extra-terrestrial was known to have taken place. Occasionally these stones bear the carved effigy of the being there encountered. There are several in Britain and examples all over the world, including Australia, where full length Wondjina portraits are found occupying each a single stone. Again, there are recent examples of this practice, including the inscribed stone monument marking the spot where Thomas the Rhymer, an ancester of Lermontov, met the fairy queen, who took him to her unearthly land.

There is no surviving dragon story at Glastonbury Tor, but an alternative legend, that of the Celtic glass tower, points its association with flying saucers of the past. A Welsh hermit of the Dark Ages, St Collen, occupied a cell in the hill. A demon appeared to him and called him to a meeting with the demon King, Gwyn, on the summit. St Collen climbed the hill and found Gwyn's castle magically transported to its peak. After conversation with Gwyn, St Collen dashed a bottle of holy water at the apparition and the demon King, his court and his tower vanished into thin air.

In 1929 a remarkable discovery in the country around Glastonbury Tor was claimed by Miss K. Maltwood and described in her book *A Guide to Glastonbury's Temple of the Stars*. Below the Tor, she says, lies a giant Zodiac arranged in a circle of diameter some ten miles. Inside the circle figures, zodiacal and legendary, are marked out on the ground by natural and artificial features, such as hills, streams, ditches, boundaries and roads. Their size is so great that they can only be detected on a large scale map and can never be seen, so that only those who knew the secret of the figures could ever suspect their existence. Miss Maltwood supports her theory with allusions to the figures in early writing and folklore, particularly to those of Arthurian legend. She suggests that the figures, which correspond to the pattern of constellations in the sky were laid out by an ancient race of astronomer-priests, and that the secret of the Zodiac was revealed only to initiates into their cult. If, as is not impossible, Richard Whiting and his two companions had inherited a knowledge of the great Zodiac, their last vision on the gallows at the top of Glaston-

146

bury Tor would have been the huge, mystical figures spread out on the plains below them.

Whether or not some great sculpted message to the sky gods does lie below Glastonbury Tor, as Miss Maltwood describes, there is no doubt that the whole area was particularly sacred to the early flying saucer cult. The dragon legend, while not now attached to the Tor itself, may have become transferred to other nearby mounds. There are several versions in other parts of Somerset. The dragon of Aller, a few miles from Glastonbury, is still remembered locally. It came out of Athelney fens and terrorised the countryside until a local man killed it with a spear. This very spear can be found in the church at Low Ham, a beautiful and lonely building which stands in a field near the place of the dragon's death. A dragon breathing fire also appeared at Kingston St Mary; another was killed by Fulk Fitzwain on the Quantocks. A sacrificial hill, Crowcombe Height, was the haunt of another Somerset dragon, the Worm of Shervage Wood, which coiled itself round the hill and devoured sheep and cattle.

The dragon is a synonym for the flying saucers, the airships of the gods, in the past; any hill or mound which features in an original dragon legend must have been one of the high places of sacrifice, where the gods received their tribute. Such hills can be found all over the country, for there are more dragon legends in Britain than any-where outside China. One of the most famous British dragons is the Lambton Worm of Durham.

This monster took up its position on a rock in the middle of the river Wear, having emerged from a nearby well. It was of hideous appearance with nine holes on each side of its mouth. So large did it grow that the rock became too small to support it and the Worm moved to a hill on the banks of the Wear and coiled itself around the summit. This hill is a typical 'worm hill', conical, flat-topped and of artificial appearance. From here the Worm devastated the country, demanding vast quantities of milk as well as sheep and cattle as a form of tribute. Finally the heir to the Lambton estates, returned from the Crusades, prepared to attack the monster. He put on a suit of armour covered in sharp blades and took up his position on an island in the Wear. The Worm coiled round him, but pierced by the blades and by the heir's sword, it fell to pieces. A property of such monsters is that, when cut up, the segments magically reunite, but in this case the swift current of the Wear prevented the pieces from finding each other, and the Worm was finally destroyed.

This is the complete British dragon legend. In all its versions certain points are emphasised, which help to explain its true significance. The monster, like the fire-bearing serpent of Ainu legend, first appears from a well or pit, having in some cases first descended from the sky. It makes for the flat top of some hill where, from its practice of coiling round the summit, it is evident that its typical form is circular. From the high place where it lives, the dragon demands sacrifice.

In all this the dragon is identified both with the modern flying saucer (the holes on each side of the mouth of the Lambton Worm were evidently the typical portholes so often seen round the flying saucers' rim) and with the old belief that the vehicles of the gods once landed on high places to demand sacrifice. It is therefore possible by an analysis of British dragon legends to discover those hills where sacrifices to the former flying saucer gods took place.

Many of them are found in the north of England and in Scotland. The Worm of Linton in Roxburghshire coiled itself round a hill now known as 'Wormistone' and by the suction of its poisonous breath drew all the local crops and cattle into its mouth. The Laird of Lariston was the hero who killed it by thrusting a lump of peat coated in burning pitch between its jaws. The Worm in its death throes scored a great spiral into the hill of the sort which can be seen at other such places including Glastonbury Tor.

A whole family of dragons inhabited Ben Vehir, a mountain near Glencoe and, until they were destroyed, preyed on all who came within reach. Another such monster infested a hill above a well at Pittempton near Dundee.

The Scottish tradition of sacrificing to serpents persisted, according to Hardwick, up to the end of the nineteenth century. Milk was left on a hillside near Loch Maree, and in the same district a bull was sacrificed on an island, an event which took place within living memory. From this it appears that the practice of making offerings to the flying saucer gods survived almost up to the time of the revival of their legend in recent years.

North of England dragons include the Pollard Worm and that of Sockburn, a 'worm, dragon or fiery flying serpent which destroyed man, woman and child'. The estate and lordship of the Manor of Sockburn, a remote and haunted spot with a ruined church and deserted village, cut off from the surrounding country by a great bend of the River Tees, was bestowed upon the hero who destroyed this monster, Sir John Conyers. He and his descendants held their possessions on condition that the sword with which the deed was done be presented to every new Bishop of Durham, who then duly returned it. This custom was last observed in 1826. The last Conyers died at the end of the nineteenth century, a pauper in Chester-le-Street. Other families, however, descendants of dragon-killing heroes, still flourish, some, like Lambton, Somerville and Venables on the lands granted to their ancestor for his feat, and some bearing on their arms the significant crest of the dragon surmounting a sky wheel.

Among some thirty surviving legends of the British dragon are those of the Laidley Worm of Spindleston Heugh, the dragon of Loschy Hill in Yorkshire, the dragon of Bromfield near Ludlow, the serpent of Denbigh Castle, the dragon of Sexhow and those of Mordiford in Herefordshire and St Osyths in Essex. A study of the whole subject is badly needed, and it would be interesting for visitors to the various dragon hills and sites of the legend to enquire whether they had been the centre of any recent flying saucer reports or rumours, as sometimes appears to have been the case.

Other hills associated with flying saucers of the past include those with a haunted reputation like Chanctonbury Ring, a place so sinister that a party of Sussex University students, who recently determined to spend the night there with cameras and tape recordings, were seized with sudden panic and fled down the hillside leaving their equipment behind them.

Another legend which distinguishes such hills is that described by Rev. J. E. Field in *The Myth of the Pent Cuckoo*. This legend, which appears in the collection of tales of the Wise Men of Gotham, tells how the village simpletons decided to make the summer last for ever. They planned to do this by stopping the cuckoo from leaving the country, so they built a wall round the crown of the hill where on a tree the cuckoo was singing. When the cuckoo flew over their wall, they declared that they had not built it high enough.

The walls, to which the story refers, turn out to be those earthworks with which so many prehistoric sacred places were surrounded and which were later used as fortresses. The cuckoo, a bird of ominous reputation, which has attracted much superstition and was itself the object of sacrifice until recently in many parts of Europe, is a fitting symbol for the visitors from the sky.

Hills associated with this legend include those of Elvington, Swyncombe, Mongewell, Elmewe and Ipsden. Many others where something of the sort took place can probably be found.

From the various dragon legends it seems clear that there once existed a religious practice consisting of the offering of sacrifice to the gods at the top of a hill. A memory of the gods who descended in circular vehicles to receive the offerings is preserved in the stories of the dragon, which, as we have seen, was the description for flying saucers in the past. For some time the dragons rested on their hill-tops levying tribute, and then they were attacked and defeated. The departure of the gods, whether of their own accord or because of battles with men, is described in the killing of the dragon, and the same myth was later adapted to illustrate the supplanting of the old religion by Christianity. This was particularly the case in Ireland where a memory of the sky gods remained strong into modern times. The story of St Patrick and his expulsion of the serpents from the holy mountain in County Mayo originated in the exploits of an earlier hero, someone such as Fionn, the Fenian leader who killed a serpent at the artificial sacred mound of Howth, and another at Lough Leary, which devoured fifty horses a day as well as many men.

Near Howth stands the great pyramid of Ireland, New Grange, about fifty feet high and a quarter of a mile in circumference, made of stones and once covered with a facing of white quartz pebbles. Now it appears as a large grassy mound. The base is ringed about with a circle of stone slabs, many of which bear the carved sign of the spinning disc in the sky, the serpent or spiral. Here was the centre of the sky god cult of Ireland, the white mountain, a conspicuous landmark from the air, where the gods made their landfall. Like White Tower Hill of London, New Grange was later used as a place of burial. In 1699 a cave consisting of a straight passage with two alcoves, the whole forming the shape of a cross, was discovered deep inside the mound, and in the cave were two skeletons. This design, the cross within the circle, found in the Celtic cross, the cruciform church placed within the pre-Christian circular graveyard and in the gold disc marked with a cross unearthed from a prehistoric Wessex tomb as well as in many other forms, appears to stand for the god inside the disc, the vessel in which he navigates the air. Graves believes that the chamber inside New Grange was at one time used to contain the oracular serpents, the objects of the Irish snake cult. Certainly the mound was erected in honour of the serpent, but it was the serpent in the sky, rather than in any earthly manifestation, which received offerings on the top of New Grange.

White Tower Hill, the mound on which the Tower of London now stands was, like New Grange, a landing place for the gods. Here was buried the oracular talisman, the head of Bran, a figure identified by Spence with the Keeper of the Grail and thence with the Grail, the flying disc, itself. Bran was killed on an expedition to Ireland, and his head, brought to Wales by his followers, kept the whole company entertained by its conversation and oracular utterances for seven years at Harlech and for eighty years more on Bardsey Island. Here they feasted and were entranced by the unearthly beauty of distant bird song, until one man did the fated forbidden thing, the spell was broken, and the head was taken for burial to White Tower Hill. From this eminence it kept watch over the safety of Britain until it was unwisely dug up by King Arthur. Whether or not this means that at one time a talisman, a flying disc was buried beneath the Tower of London, the Tower certainly maintained its role as a place of sacrifice. The White Tower, the holy meeting place between men and gods, became the Bloody Tower where executions repeated the cult of human sacrifice which itself had distorted the original meaning of contact with the gods.

Around the southern half of the circumference of New Grange, at some distance from the base stands a semi-circle of stones. The combination of the circle and the semi-circle or horseshoe shape seen also in the enigmatic cup and ring marks on rocks all over Britain and in parts of Europe, appears to stand for the people from the sky, the helmeted gods and their aircraft. In Genesis IX is the story of how God set the rainbow in the sky to mark his covenant with Noah, that men should henceforth live under his protection. Here the inverted horseshoe is revealed as the emblem of the divine race, a perpetual reminder to men of the gods and of the laws or covenant they had once established on earth for men's benefit.

'And the bow shall be in the cloud; and I will look upon it, that I may remember the everlasting covenant between God and every living creature of all flesh that is upon the earth.'

The Wondjina, the gods from the sky who first established the laws

151

of men, appear in Australian painted caves wearing over their heads the inverted horseshoe. So do the god-figures carved thousands of years ago on the rocks of Mexico, South America and Central Asia. In this symbol of the superior race can also be seen the origin of the halo. On the rock walls placed in relationship with the Wondjina appears the figure of the rainbow serpent, arching his back protectively over the world in exactly the same way as Nut, the Egyptian goddess of the dead. The rainbow serpent also figures in the mythology of the Indians of the west coast of America. The inverted horseshoe shape of the rainbow serpent demonstrates a reversal of the more usual process by which, from representing the vehicle of the gods, the snake came to stand for the gods themselves. In this case the horseshoe symbol of the men from the sky became the symbol of their vehicle, the serpent.

The great inverted horseshoe within the circle of Stonehenge was a display of their own sign to the gods in the sky. Its meaning was retained in the popular superstitions involving horseshoes. To nail them upright over the door of a house was, by reversing their sign, to deny the old gods, to commit a blasphemy in the same way that to stick a postage stamp upside down on a letter is considered by some to be an insult to the Queen. This was done to keep out evil spirits, a renunciation of degenerate vestiges of a memory of the alien race. Their symbol, the inverted horseshoe came to be a sign of ill omen.

The memory of the former gods and their circular airships, contained in the cult of the serpent or dragon, also inspired the building of certain remarkable monuments in the form of spiralled earth mounds as a sign to the people in the sky. Like the lines on the Nazca plains and the White Horse in Berkshire, these monuments only have any meaning when viewed from above. Like Avebury, which Stukely saw as the outline of a great winged globe or serpent (a view reflected in the medieval stone carving in Avebury Church showing a struggle between a bishop and a pair of dragons) they are in the shape of serpents. These serpent mounds are sometimes of enormous size and are built of earth. The most famous are those of America. An earth mound in Adams County, Ohio, built on a hill, is in the form of a partly coiled serpent, its jaws open to swallow some globular object. It is 1,348 feet long, its body is thirty feet wide and the whole figure is about five feet high. Other serpent mounds in Iowa extend over two miles; one by St Peter's River is 2,310 feet long.

These impressive monuments to the serpent in the sky are related to smaller but comparable structures in Britain. Serpent mounds have been found in Scotland. In Argyllshire the remains of an earth serpent of great size stands on the banks of the Clyde. At Glen Feochan by Loch Nell near Oban is another about 300 feet long and twenty feet high, and there is a coiled serpent mound at Ach-na-Goul near Inveraray. These mounds on both sides of the Atlantic provide the most explicit illustration of the cult of the coiled sky serpent or flying disc in former times.

Although it was usually on the hilltops that men came into contact with the gods, there are other places, still invested with a reputation for sanctity, where some revelation of the gods to men may once have taken place. These places, marked and enclosed by stone circles, appear to have an inherent quality which distinguishes them from others. The number of visitors to the sites of stone circles seems quite out of proportion to the picturesque qualities of the stones themselves. It is as if the actual sites still possess some attraction which makes them naturally sympathetic. The Rollright Stones in Oxfordshire, by no means large or impressive in themselves are always surrounded by visitors, and pilgrims. A common practice is for people to walk round the circumference of the circle, counting the stones. The popular story here, as at many other British stone circles, is that the stones cannot accurately be counted, for one always arrives at a different figure each time. This legend may well be a memory of past rites at the site, involving a procession round the stones.

A reason for the peculiarly attractive qualities which the sites of stone circles possess may be seen in some of the legend and folklore in which they are so rich. Often the stones are said to be petrified people; 'the Hurlers', a Cornish circle, are men who played games on the Sabbath, and other Cornish groups like 'the Nine Maids' of Stithians as well as the stones of Stanton Drew in Somerset represent dancers also petrified for Sabbath breaking. These stories certainly refer to rites carried out at stone circles. The memory of what form they took has survived, for the practice of worship at stone circles may have continued in the same way up to the present time. It may be perpetuated today in the meetings of witch covens which still take place at stone circles on Dartmoor and maybe elsewhere in the country.

There seems, therefore, to be an authentic tradition that the rites at stone circles took the form of circular dancing. What lay behind this practice may be seen in a legend of the Rollright Stones, according to which the stones rise into the air at midnight and spin round above the site where they normally stand. Here again is the belief in a spinning disc in the sky, a belief also illustrated by the old country tale that the sun dances in the sky early on Easter morning. Another Rollright legend that the stones are the petrified figures of an invading King and his army, reveals a traditional association of the site with a powerful, alien race. It is likely, therefore, that at Rollright and elsewhere the stone circles were erected to commemorate a vision of a spinning disc and the descent of its occupants.

The conclusion that can be drawn from the evidence of the legends and prehistoric monuments of Britain is that the form which obsessed

ROLLRIGHT STONES

Fig. 6 The Rollright Stones

the early inhabitants and inspired their worship was the spinning disc in the sky. This object is revealed in several ways. First in the legend of the dragon which clings to so many of the high places, the sacrificial tables of the gods. The dragon and the sky disc are, as has been shown, identical objects. Secondly, the flying saucer cult can be seen in the shape of certain monuments of antiquity, such as Stonehenge, a structure which accurately reproduces the flying saucer as it is said to appear today. Other stone circles have legends describing the stones rising up and gyrating in the air. On certain stones, particularly those of New Grange, the sacred pyramid of the sky gods, are found symbols of the objects of worship, the carved spirals which represent the whirling disc in the sky. A third piece of evidence for the existence in antiquity of a flying saucer cult is the Celtic coast of Britain sacred to the dead and to the cult of sacrifice. Another version of the glass towers are the glass boats of mythology and fairy legend. The story that they travelled with equal ease over land and sea indicates that they were flying vessels, like the flying ship filled with warriors in the legend of St Columba. Sometimes the enchanted towers contained the beautiful queen of a divine race, a figure of Celtic mythology whom A. B. Cook compares to the Magician, Kirke. Her name, associating her with the circle, is appropriate to the vehicle which conveyed her through the air, the flying disc legend of the revolving glass towers. These seem to have been the strongholds and also the vehicles of the gods, appearing on the high places and particularly on those small islands off the west described as a team of serpents. Another such vessel, a glass boat, conveyed the Celtic hero, Conla the Red, to the land of fairies, vanishing into the West as a glowing disc of ever-changing colour.

At one time it was generally held that the sky disc as an object of worship referred to a solar cult. In fact there is no doubt that after the departure of the gods, the memory of their flying discs was embodied in the symbol of the sun. But sun worship was only a corruption of an earlier cult, that of the flying saucer. This can be seen in the central object of British mythology, the cauldron or Grail. This vessel has a legend, similar to that of the serpent, the vehicle of the gods. It belongs to another world, and sometimes itself stands for the unearthly country; it inspires men with wisdom, and reveals to them great secrets, raising them to the level of the gods; it heals wounds, bestows immortality, gives to everyone what he wants most. Here is another version of the legend of the flying saucer, the vehicle by which the gods with their advanced culture first made themselves known. The Grail was the sacred vessel, once known on earth but now removed to another world from which it may occasionally reappear to be glimpsed by men until the day when it is finally attracted to earth again. It was the vehicle by which all benefits first came to men, the flying disc of the gods.

As King Arthur's Knights of the Round Table were seated in the hall at Camelot, the Holy Grail appeared overhead. A clap of thunder sounded, a bright light shone forth, the hall became filled with a beautiful scent and colours played on the faces of all the Knights, so that they became transformed and every one appeared radiant to his neighbour. At that moment the food and drink of all those at the table became that which they most liked. Then the Grail and its attendant entered the hall. Covered in white samite it passed overhead and disappeared. Immediately all the knights swore to dedicate their lives to the quest for this sublime object.

This vision was so similar to the flying saucer visitation at Fatima that the real identity of the Grail must be evident. At Fatima the disc spun, terrifyingly beautiful, overhead. Fantastic colours illuminated the landscape and glowed in the faces of the great crowd of watchers. It was a moment of magical inspiration, the coming of the Holy Ghost. As at Camelot the maiden who accompanied the luminous globe at Fatima was half seen by a few of those who witnessed the vision. Evidently she was the same woman of unearthly race who appears as the 'swan-maiden' in flying saucer mythology and inspired the visions of such modern prophets as Howard Menger.

The Holy Grail, as presented in Malory's collection of Arthurian legends, appears in the form of a Christian relic, the cup from the Last Supper, brought to England by Joseph of Arimathea. But the Grail cult is far older than Christianity. Taliesin, the Welsh bard, recorded the legend of King Arthur and his companions invading an unearthly country to capture the cauldron of Annwn. This vessel was fired by the breath of nine maidens. Wisdom in oracular form issued from it, and it would provide no food for cowards. Around the rim of the cauldron was set a row of pearls. This feature tends to identify it with the inyx wheel of the sky gods which, like flying saucers of today, appears in illustrations with a circle of dots around its circumference. The same figure can be seen in a stone carving in Brinsop Church, Herefordshire, another site of St George's defeat of the dragon.

The cauldron of Annwn, the early version of the Holy Grail, reappears in the Welsh legend from the Mabinogion as the cauldron of Keridwen. She was a goddess with three children, one of whom was so ugly that she wanted to compensate him with the gift of inspiration. In her cauldron she brewed a mixture of herbs from which at the end of a year three drops of the inspiring potion would be distilled. A servant boy, Gwion, was posted to guard the cauldron. At the end of the year, as he was stirring it, the mixture bubbled up and three drops flew onto his thumb and burnt it. Gwion thrust his thumb into his mouth and was immediately inspired. He recognised the underlying patterns of the universe and understood the language of the birds. In fact he entered that state outside time, which Australian Aborigines call the dream-time, the plain on which, they say, lives a people formerly known on earth in the days when the language of animals could be understood by men.

The Christian Grail was something more remote and ethereal. It was no longer known to men on earth and some aspects of its nature had been forgotten. But on the occasions when it reappeared, men were reminded of the golden age, the days when the gods were openly known. Only those worthy of the vision saw the beautiful object. Tennyson's poem describes how it appeared to the nun, Sir Percivale's sister.

> ' . . . and then
> Stream'd thro' my cell a cold and silver beam,
> And down the long beam stole the Holy Grail,
> Rose red with beatings on it as if alive,
> Till all the white walls of my cell were dyed
> With rosy colours leaping on the wall.'

Even in this late version, the identity of the Grail is not hard to perceive. King Arthur was the last of a line of rulers who had tried to preserve something of the culture which had been established in the days of the gods. His adviser, Merlin, was descended from the superior race and from his father knew many of their secrets. Merlin finally left earth, rejoining his people in the traditional way by entering a tower. Arthur's father, Uther Pendragon, had taken for his badge the dragon, the flying saucer symbol, and in Malory's account Arthur, on succeeding to the Kingdom, dreamed of freeing the country of serpents and dragons. The quest for the Grail, which the Knights of the Round Table undertook, was an attempt to recapture the vision of the disc in the sky, to attract back to earth the gods who had deserted it.

From being known as the vehicle of the gods, the Grail came, like the dragon, to stand for the gods themselves and for their possessions which set them above men. Particularly coveted was their food, which in the eyes of men was the source of their immortality. The disc from the sky was the vessel which contained this food, and hence it became thought of as a cup or cauldron. The worship of the gods led to the cult of a holy vessel. Cups and bowls were made as objects of the cult, and several have survived into modern times, still with their sanctity and their priest. One such is the vessel called the Luck of Edenhall in Cumberland. It is a goblet about six inches high, made of greenish glass with a device in blue and white enamel picked out in gold and crimson. The Musgraves preserved it on account of a tradition which says that the cup was stolen from the fairies by a butler many centuries ago. As the man made off with their cup the fairies cried,

> *If the glass do break or fall*
> *Farewell the luck of Edenhall.'*

The Musgraves therefore became the hereditary guardians of one of the last relics of the original flying saucer cult, the symbol of the Grail.

CHAPTER NINE

Conclusion

Hitherto all the theories of modern scholarship have, as Lenin observed, been based on the assumption that we are alone in the universe. The possibility that our whole development has been influenced by extra-terrestrial forces, with which we may again have to reckon some time in the future, is still hardly considered. Yet, as we have seen, this idea lay behind all the study and religious observances of antiquity. Our disregard for life outside the earth is something new, an attitude which we may not be able for much longer to maintain.

The reappearance of flying saucers and our reawakening interest in extra-terrestrial life represents, therefore, a return to an orthodoxy temporarily abandoned. The object of this book has been first to establish the existence in the past of a flying saucer cult and to examine its origins; secondly to suggest some of the ways in which the revival of our belief in these objects is likely to affect us in the years to come. In attempting this a great deal of material has been included which may, perhaps, seem irrelevant, over-elaborate or even contradictory. The excuse for this is that so little has up to now been written on the subject and so impossible is it to foresee the nature of the changes which our recognition of extra-terrestrial life will bring, that the field for speculation is almost limitless, and it is hard to know where to place the emphasis.

The changed conditions, which we are already beginning to have to face, will necessitate a reassessment of the fundamentals of every branch of science and knowledge. There is urgent work to be done in every field. Only by analysing the influence of the early knowledge of flying saucers and the gods upon the structure of ancient societies can we find some clue to the probable effects of our confrontation with them in the future. It is essential that the true basis of mythology be recognised and the origins of our civilisation examined in the light of what we can now suspect of extra-terrestrial influences in the past.

The ancient symbols for the gods and their airships must be recognised for what they are, and a plan made of the places on earth with which they were once closely associated. From this study a pattern will emerge to accord with and explain the modern phenomena which are causing so much anxiety and uncertainty. If we can accept that the appearance of flying saucers and extra-terrestrial life is nothing new, but something which has been known in the past, perhaps a part of a regular cycle or pattern which our civilisation is not yet old enough to have recorded, we may be able to avoid the ultimate disasters which our sudden confrontation with people from space may cause.

Books Consulted

Flying Saucers and Similar Subjects

ADAMSKI, GEORGE AND LESLIE, DESMOND: *Flying Saucers Have Landed.* T. Werner Laurie Ltd. London, 1953.

ANGELUCCI, ORFEO: *The Secret of the Saucers.* Amherst Press. Wisconsin, 1955.

BENDER, ALBERT K.: *Flying Saucers and the Three Men.* Saucerian Books. Clarksville, W. Va., 1962.

—— *Flying Saucer Review.* London. All issues since 1955.

GIBBONS, GAVIN: *They Rode in Space Ships.* Neville Spearman. London, 1957.

JESSUP, M.K.: *The Case for the U.F.O.s.* Arco Publications Ltd. London, 1956.

—— *The Expanding Case for the U.F.O.s.* Arco Publications Ltd. London, 1957.

KEYHOE, MAJOR DONALD: *The Flying Saucer Conspiracy.* Hutchinson. London, 1957.

MENGER, HOWARD: *From Outer Space to You.* Saucerian Books. Clarksville, W. Va., 1959.

MICHEL, AIMÉ: *The Truth about Flying Saucers.* Robert Hale Ltd. London, 1957.

—— *Flying Saucers and the Straight Line Mystery.* Criterion Books. New York, 1958.

PHILIP, BROTHER: *The Secret of the Andes.* Neville Spearman. London, 1961.

VALLÉE, JACQUES: *Anatomy of a Phenomenon.* Henry Regnery Co. Chicago, 1966.

WILKINS, HAROLD T.: *Flying Saucers Uncensored.* Arco Publications Ltd. London, 1956.

General Subjects

ALLCROFT, A. HADRIAN: *The Circle and the Cross.* Macmillan & Co. London, 1917.

ASHE, GEOFFREY: *King Arthur's Avalon.* Collins. London, 1957.

ATKINSON, R. J. C.: *Stonehenge.* Hamish Hamilton. London, 1956.

BATCHELOR, REV. J.: *The Ainu and their Folklore.*

BERNHEIMER, RICHARD: *Wild Men in the Middle Ages.* Harvard Univ. Press. Cambridge, Mass., 1955.

BONWICK, JAMES: *Irish Druids and the Old Irish Religion.* Griffith, Farran & Co. London, 1894.

BARING-GOULD, REV. S.: *Curious Myths of the Middle Ages.* Rivingtons. London, 1868.

—— *Historical Oddities and Strange Events.* Methuen. London, 1889.

BLACKETT, W. S.: *The Lost Histories of America.* Trübner & Co. London, 1883.

BRIGGS, K. M.: *Pale Hecate's Team.* Routledge & Kegan Paul. London, 1959.

————— *The Anatomy of Puck*. Routledge & Kegan Paul. London, 1962.

CLEVELAND, DUCHESS OF: *The True Story of Kaspar Hauser*. Macmillan & Co. London, 1893.

COOK, A. B.: *Zeus*. Cambridge Univ. Press, 1914.

COWAN, JAMES: *Fairy Folk Tales of the Maori*. Whitcombe & Tombs Ltd. London, 1935.

CAMPBELL, J.: *The Masks of God, Primitive Mythology*. Secker & Warburg. London, 1960.

DAVIDSON, D. S.: *Aboriginal Australian Rock Carvings and Paintings*. American Philosophical Society, Philadelphia, 1936.

EMERSON, E. R.: *Indian Myths*. Trübner & Co. London, 1885.

EVANS, ELIZABETH E.: *The Story of Kaspar Hauser*. Swan Sonnenschein & Co. London, 1892.

FEUERBACH, A. VON: *Caspar Hauser*. Simpkin & Marshall. London. 1834.

FIELD, REV. J.: *The Myth of the Pent Cuckoo*. Elliot Stock. London, 1913.

GIBBS-SMITH, C. H.: *The History of Flying*. C. T. Batsford Ltd. London, 1953.

GRAVES, R.: *The White Goddess*. Faber & Faber Ltd. London, 1948.

————— *Greek Myths*. Penguin Books. London, 1955.

GREGORY, LADY: *Visions and Beliefs in the West of Ireland*. G. P. Putnams Sons. New York, 1920.

GUEST, LADY CHARLOTTE: *The Mabinogion*, 1849.

HARTLAND, E. S.: *The Science of Fairy Tales*. Methuen & Co. Ltd. London, 1925.

HAWKINS, GERALD S.: *Stonehenge Decoded*. Souvenir Press. London, 1966.

HAYES, L. N.: *The Chinese Dragon*. Commercial Press Ltd. Shanghai, 1923.

HENDERSON, W.: *Notes on the Folklore of the Northern Counties of England*. London, 1866.

HIPPISLEY COX, R.: *The Green Roads of England*. Methuen & Co. London, 1914.

HOMET, M.: *On The Trial of the Sun Gods*. Neville Spearman. London, 1965.

HONORÉ, P.: *In Quest of the White God*. Hutchinson. London, 1963.

IDRIESS, ION L.: *Our Living Stone Age*. Angus & Robertson Ltd. London, 1964.

JENNINGS, H.: *Curious Things*. T. & W. Boone, London, 1861.

JUNG, C. J.: *Flying Saucers. A Modern Myth of Things Seen in the Skies*. Routledge & Kegan Paul. London, 1959.

KENDRICK, T. D.: *The Druids*. Methuen & Co. Ltd. London, 1927.

KERENYI, K.: *Prometheus*. Rhein-Verlag. Zürich, 1946.

KIRK, R.: *The Secret Commonwealth*. M.S. 1691. Eneas Mackay. Stirling, 1933.

LAUFER, BERTHOLD: *The Prehistory of Aviation*. Field Columbian Museum, 1928.

LELAND, C. G.: *Algonkin Legends of New England*. Boston Houghton, Mifflin & Co. New York, 1884.

LHOTE, HENRI: *The Search for the Tassili Frescoes*. Hutchinson. London, 1959.

LOCKHART, J. G.: *Mysteries of the Sea*. Philip Allan & Co. London, 1924.

————— *Strange Adventures of the Sea*. Philip Allan & Co. London, 1925.

MACGREGOR, ALASDAIR ALPIN: *Behold the Hebrides*. W. R. Chambers Ltd. London, 1925.

————— *The Haunted Isles*. Alexander Maclehose & Co. London, 1933.

MACKENZIE, DONALD A.: *Myths of Pre-Columbian America*. The Gresham Publishing Co. Ltd. London, 1926.

162

—— *Scottish Folk-Lore and Folk-Life*. Blackie & Son. London, 1935.

MACKENZIE, W. C.: *The Book of the Lews*. Alexander Gardner. Paisley, 1919.

—— *The Western Isles*. Alexander Gardner. Paisley, 1932.

MACRITCHIE, D.: *The Testament of Tradition*. Kegan Paul, Trench, Trübner & Co. London, 1890.

MALTWOOD, K. E.: *A Guide to Glastonbury's Temple of the Stars*. James Clarke & Co. Ltd. London, 1929.

MARTIN, M.: *A Description of the Western Islands of Scotland*. A. Bell & others. London, 1716.

MOORE, PATRICK: *Guide to Mars*. Frederick Muller Ltd. London, 1965.

MURRAY, MARGARET: *The God of the Witches*. Sampson Low, Marston & Co. Ltd. London, 1933.

O'NEILL, JOHN: *The Night of the Gods*. Bernard Quaritch, 1893.

O'RÍORDÁIN, SEAN P. AND DANIEL, GLYN.: *New Grange*. Thames & Hudson, London.

PAUWELS, LOUIS AND BERGIER, JACQUES: *The Dawn of Magic*. Anthony Gibbs & Phillips. London, 1963.

PIGGOTT, STUART: *William Stukeley*. Clarendon Press. Oxford, 1950.

RAGLAN, LORD: *The Hero*. Methuen & Co. Ltd. London, 1936.

SIKES, WIRT: *British Goblins*. James R. Osgood & Co. Boston, 1881.

SINNETT, A. P.: *Stonehenge and the Pyramids*. The Theosophical Publishing House, London Ltd., 1893.

SMITH, G. ELLIOT: *The Evolution of the Dragon*. The Univ. Press, Manchester and Longmans, Green & Co. London, 1919.

SOUSTELLE, JACQUES: *The Daily Life of the Aztecs on the Eve of the Spanish Conquest*. Weidenfeld & Nicolson. London, 1961.

SPENCE, LEWIS: *The Gods of Mexico*. T. Fisher Unwin Ltd. London, 1923.

—— *Mysteries of Britain*. Rider & Co. London, 1928.

—— *The Fairy Tradition in Britain*. Rider & Co. London, 1948.

—— *The Minor Traditions of British Mythology*. Rider & Co. London, 1948.

—— *Magic Arts in Celtic Britain*. Rider & Co. London, 1945.

—— *Atlantis in America*. Ernest Benn. London, 1925.

SQUIRE, C.: *Mythology of the British Islands*. Blackie & Son Ltd. London, 1905.

STANHOPE, LORD: *Tracts Relating to Kaspar Hauser*. James S. Hodson. London, 1836.

STEWART, OLIVER: *Danger in the Air*. Routledge & Kegan Paul. London, 1958.

SUMMERS, REV. MONTAGUE: *The History of Witchcraft & Demonology*. Kegan Paul, Trench, Trübner & Co. Ltd. London, 1926.

TEILHARD DE CHARDIN, P.: *The Phenomenon of Man*. Collins. London, 1959.

TENNYSON, ALFRED LORD: *The Holy Grail*.

WATKINS, A.: *Early British Trackways*. Simpkin, Marshall & Co. London, 1922.

—— *The Old Straight Track*. Methuen & Co. Ltd. London, 1925.

WERNER, ALICE: *Myths and Legends of the Bantu*. G. G. Harrap & Co. London, 1933.

WILLS, WILLIAM JOHN: *A Successful Exploration through the Interior of Australia*. Richard Bentley. London, 1863.

Index

166

THE VIEW OVER ATLANTIS

JOHN MICHELL

A revolutionary theory of prehistoric civilisation, already established as an 'underground' classic.

75p

CITY OF REVELATION

JOHN MICHELL

A fascinating examination of the numerical formula that was the essence of the sacred canon of the peoples of prehistory. 'John Michell is a genius ... short-circuiting established channels of thought and offering a brilliant network of his own.'
Time Out

50p

THE SACRED MUSHROOM AND THE CROSS

JOHN M. ALLEGRO

'Allegro boldly sketches in the origins of the primitive fertility cult .... It is a dazzling foray into the obscure hinterland of comparative philology.'
Dennis Potter, The Times

60p

WORLDS IN COLLISION

IMMANUEL VELIKOVSKY

'Fascinating . . . in its stupendous pictures of a world in the grip of cosmic forces, in its parallels drawn from the annals of the ancients in many lands, and in its vast implications.'
Oxford Mail

60p

EARTH IN UPHEAVAL

IMMANUEL VELIKOVSKY

'Velikovsky abandons the literary and the legendary. He goes into the fields of astronomy, archaeology, geology and biology . . . to cast serious doubt on all kinds of accepted hypotheses in these various fields.'
Diogenes, Time and Tide

60p

AGES IN CHAOS

IMMANUEL VELIKOVSKY

Dr Velikovsky reconstructs the political and cultural histories of the nations of the ancient world to present a unique and radical revision of ancient history.

75p Illustrated

POETRY DIMENSION 1

Edited by JEREMY ROBSON

The first truly comprehensive look at the current poetry scene, which highlights the best poetry and the best prose about poetry published in books and magazines over the past twelve months.

75p

THE PARADE'S GONE BY . . .

KEVIN BROWNLOW

The classic and acclaimed work on Hollywood during the 'golden age' between 1912 and the advent of sound sixteen years later.

£1·75 Illustrated

STANLEY KUBRICK DIRECTS

ALEXANDER WALKER

Richly illustrated with over 350 stills, which add force to the detailed analyses of style and content, this book traces the flow of Kubrick's work from *Paths of Glory* to *Dr Strangelove, 2001: A Space Odyssey,* and *A Clockwork Orange.*

£1·00 Illustrated

BLACK ELK SPEAKS

The Life Story of a Holy Man of the Oglala Sioux as told to JOHN G. NEIHARDT

'A beautiful and eloquent testament to the dream of a way of life that died with a people in defeat.'
The Cork Examiner

90p Illustrated

THE BOOK ON THE TABOO AGAINST KNOWING WHO YOU ARE

ALAN WATTS

'This lovely and humorous work will shock, outrage, excite, delight and profoundly stimulate anyone who has ever asked "Who or What am I?".'
Irish Press

45p

GETTING BACK TOGETHER

ROBERT HOURIET

'A charged and comprehensive report on American communes that is also an odyssey, one man's confession ... It's difficult not to be moved.'
Cosmopolitan

75p Illustrated

SONG AND DANCE MAN

MICHAEL GRAY

'The best Dylan study yet – with massive quotation from his lyrics and a careful balance held in assessment of his work.'
Sunday Times

75p Illustrated

ELVIS

JERRY HOPKINS

'Just about as comprehensive a book as anyone is ever likely to offer on a pop idol. This is exactly the book which legions of Presley fans throughout the world will clamour for.'
Evening News

£1·00 Illustrated

MICK JAGGER

J. MARKS

An original and powerful portrait of one of the most phenomenal performers of our age.

60p Illustrated

MUNBY: MAN OF TWO WORLDS

DEREK HUDSON

'Most extraordinary . . . a love match, a double life, a secret marriage and the eventual posthumous publication of these superbly edited diaries: an astonishing book.'
Michael Foot, Evening Standard

£1·60 Illustrated

ONE DIMENSIONAL MAN

HERBERT MARCUSE

'The most subversive book published in the United States this century.'
Le Nouvel Observateur

45p

SEXUALS POLITICS

KATE MILLETT

'The seminal book in the struggle for Women's Rights. Supremely interesting . . . brilliantly conceived.'
New York Times

60p